Follow That Girl

Julian Slade and
Dorothy Reynolds

A Samuel French Acting Edition

SAMUELFRENCH-LONDON.CO.UK
SAMUELFRENCH.COM

Copyright © Acting Edition 1967 by Julian Slade
Copyright © Music and Lyrics 1967 by Francis, Day and Hunter
All Rights Reserved

FOLLOW THAT GIRL is fully protected under the copyright laws of the British Commonwealth, including Canada, the United States of America, and all other countries of the Copyright Union. All rights, including professional and amateur stage productions, recitation, lecturing, public reading, motion picture, radio broadcasting, television and the rights of translation into foreign languages are strictly reserved.

ISBN 978-0-573-08037-1

www.samuelfrench-london.co.uk

www.samuelfrench.com

For Amateur Production Enquiries

United Kingdom and World
excluding north america
plays@SamuelFrench-London.co.uk
020 7255 4302/01

Each title is subject to availability from Samuel French,
depending upon country of performance.

CAUTION: Professional and amateur producers are hereby warned that FOLLOW THAT GIRL is subject to a licensing fee. Publication of this play does not imply availability for performance. Both amateurs and professionals considering a production are strongly advised to apply to the appropriate agent before starting rehearsals, advertising, or booking a theatre. A licensing fee must be paid whether the title is presented for charity or gain and whether or not admission is charged.

The professional rights in this play are controlled by The Agency Ltd, 24 Pottery Lane, Holland Park, London W11 4lZ.

No one shall make any changes in this title for the purpose of production. No part of this book may be reproduced, stored in a retrieval system, or transmitted in any form, by any means, now known or yet to be invented, including mechanical, electronic, photocopying, recording, videotaping, or otherwise, without the prior written permission of the publisher. No one shall upload this title, or part of this title, to any social media websites.

The right of Julian Slade and Dorothy Reynolds to be identified as author of this work has been asserted by them in accordance with Section 77 of the Copyright, Designs and Patents Act 1988

FOLLOW THAT GIRL

Presented by Linnit and Dunfee Ltd, by arrangement with J. A. Gatti, at the Vaudeville Theatre, London, on the 17th March 1960, with the following cast of characters:

TOM, the Author; afterwards Constable Blenkinsop	*Peter Gilmore*
VICTORIA	*Susan Hampshire*
MR GILCHRIST, Victoria's father	*James Cairncross*
MRS GILCHRIST, Victoria's mother	*Patricia Routledge*
TANCRED } business men, Victoria's suitors	*Philip Guard*
WILBERFORCE	*Robert McBain*
WALTER MISKIN, R.A.	*Newton Blick*
CORA MISKIN, his wife	*Marion Grimaldi*
AQUARIUM KEEPER	*James Cairncross*
MERCIA }	*Bridget Armstrong*
MAVIS } Three Mermaids	*Grazina Frame*
MAUDE }	*Betty Wood*
MISS PAYTON	*Elizabeth Henry*
EFFIE	*Grazina Frame*
EDWARD	*John Morley*
BUSMAN }	*John Baddeley*
TRAINMAN } Four Transport Officials	*John Davidson*
TUBEMAN }	*John Morley*
TAXIMAN }	*David Ryder*

PASSERS-BY, etc.   Bridget Armstrong, Grazina Frame, Anne Grayson,
Elizabeth Henry, Betty Wood
Edward Argent, John Baddeley, John Davidson,
Bernard Dickerson, John Morley, David Ryder

Directed by DENIS CAREY

Musical Numbers staged by BASIL PATTISON

Scenery and Costumes designed by HUTCHINSON SCOTT

Orchestration by PHILIP MARTELL

Lighting by RICHARD PILBROW

SYNOPSIS OF SCENES

The action passes in the Author's flat, today, and in various parts of London in late Victorian days

ACT I

SCENE 1   The Author's London Flat, a spring evening
SCENE 2   The Gilchrist Drawing-room, late 1890's
SCENE 3   Streets of London Running Tabs
SCENE 4   Battersea Park
SCENE 5   Streets of London Running Tabs
SCENE 6   Albert Bridge
SCENE 7   The Aquarium at London Zoo
SCENE 8   The City Centre

ACT II

SCENE 1A   The Author's Flat
SCENE 1B   Streets of London Running Tabs
SCENE 2   Inside Tancred's Store, Kensington
SCENE 3   Outside the Store
SCENE 4A   The Author's Flat
SCENE 4B   Transport Drop-Cloth
SCENE 5   Streets of London Running Tabs
SCENE 6   The City Centre
SCENE 7   Streets of London Running Tabs
SCENE 8   The Gilchrist Drawing-room
SCENE 9   The City Centre (Finale Cloth)

MUSIC

ACT I

No.		
	Overture and opening music	
1	"Tra, La, La"	Tom, Victoria, and Full Company
2	"Where Shall I Find My Love?"	Mrs Gilchrist, Tancred, Wilberforce, and Mr Gilchrist
3	Chase Music	
4	"I'm Away"	Walter, Cora, and Bystanders
5	"Follow That Girl"	Tom
6	Reprise, Chase Music	
7	"Solitary Stranger"	Cora, Walter, Tom, and Bystanders
8	"Victoria, Victoria"	Tancred, Wilbeforce, Cora, Mrs Gilchrist, and Chorus
9	"Lost, Stolen or Strayed"	The Bystanders
10	"Three Victorian Mermaids"	Mercia, Mavis, and Maud
11	"Mermaid Scales"	Victoria and the Aquarium Keeper
12	"Song and Dance"	Tom, Walter, Mrs Gilchrist, Tancred, Wilberforce, and Full Company

ACT II

	Opening music	
13	"Let's Take a Stroll"	Tancred, Wilberforce, and Company
14	Reprise, "Follow That Girl"	Tancred, Wilberforce, Tom, and Company
14A	Reprise, Chase Music	
15	"Shopping in Kensington"	Cora and Walter
16	"Taken for a Ride"	Victoria, Busman, Trainman, Tubeman, and Taximan
17	"Lovely Meeting You at Last"	Tom, Victoria and Chorus
18	Reprise, The Long Chase	

No.		
19	"Waiting For Our Daughter"	MR GILCHRIST and MRS GILCHRIST
20	Reprise, The End of the Chase	
21	Reprise, "Victoria, Victoria"	FULL COMPANY
22	"Wilbertan Soap Commercial"	TANCRED, WILBERFORCE, and COMPANY
23	Reprise, "Lovely Meeting You at Last"	TOM, VICTORIA, and FULL COMPANY
24	"Evening in London"	TOM, VICTORIA, and FULL COMPANY

CURTAIN CALLS

1	"Song and Dance"	THE COMPANY
2	"Solitary Stranger"	THE COMPANY
3	"Follow That Girl"	THE COMPANY

ACT I

Scene i

Scene—*The London flat of a young author; a spring evening, quite recently. A gauze drop, with black backing, is hung well down stage. It is painted to suggest that the author, Tom, is easy-going, perhaps rather untidy, and is still waiting for fame and fortune. It may well be that his flat is high under the eaves of the building, and that the ceiling painted on the gauze slopes from up R towards C. Standing on the stage down R is the only item of furniture visible; a comfortable old armchair with wide, well-padded arms.*

When the Curtain *rises, a spotlight reveals* Tom *lounging in the armchair. He is dressed casually and comfortably, and is working on a script which is messy and contains many loose pages.* Tom *hums, scribbles a note, hums again. Deep in thought he rises and takes a few steps* C. *Suddenly he looks up from his script in surprise as* Victoria *enters* L. *She is wearing a light coat and a scarf over a dress and jewellery suitable for a dinner party. The dress should be cool and close-fitting, for she will shortly have to put on her period costume over it.*

Tom. Victoria!

(Victoria *crosses excitedly to* Tom *and hugs him, script and all*)

Victoria (*panting and exultant*) I've got away!

(Tom *is delighted, but has some difficulty juggling with the script as he tries to keep hold of it and embrace Victoria at the same time*)

Tom. Isn't it tonight—your father's big business dinner?

(Victoria *releases* Tom *and crosses to* R *of the armchair*)

Victoria. Yes, seven-thirty. (*She takes off her scarf and puts it on the back of the chair*)

Tom (*turning to her, as he straightens the script*) It's seven-forty-five, and you promised him you'd be obliging.

Victoria (*sitting on* R *arm of chair*) I did mean to be. (*She unbuttons her coat*) Look, I was all got up ready to receive and a row blew up between father and me, so I fled! Rather dramatically, I thought.

Tom (*moving to* L *of the armchair*) What was the row about?

Victoria. The usual. I said his business friends were boring so he said it was time I stopped associating with a lot of scruffy authors.

Tom (*sitting on* L *arm of chair*) A lot?

Victoria. Meaning you.

Tom. I'm not scruffy. (*He puts down the script on the seat between them*)

VICTORIA. Your hair is a bit.
TOM. Is that what he's got against me—the way I do my hair?
VICTORIA (*picking up the script*) Oh, when you've had a success he'll think you're Yul Brynner. (*She settles herself in the armchair and opens the script*)
TOM (*moving round behind the chair*) Well, it won't be long now.
VICTORIA (*turning pages*) How's the show? (*She begins to read*)
TOM (*on the R of the chair*) Nearly finished. Had the boring friends begun to arrive?
VICTORIA (*her attention half on the script*) Oh, no, that would've been rude!
TOM. Why go back at all?
VICTORIA (*looking up*) What?
TOM (*urgently; crouching on his haunches beside the chair*) Why go back at all.
VICTORIA (*protesting*) Tom . . . !
TOM. Stay here. We could get married if necessary.
VICTORIA. Oh, Tom, not again! (*She is arrested by his earnest expression, and tenderly touches his cheek*) I'll see.
TOM. Are you waiting till I'm a success too?
VICTORIA. That's a horrible thing to say! You don't mean it?
TOM. No. (*He kisses her*)
VICTORIA (*after a moment, gently pushing him away*) No, not now.
TOM. Why not?
VICTORIA. This is your working evening and I don't like women who interrupt a man's work. Let's get on with it! (*She purposefully studies the script again*)
TOM. So long as you'll stay. (*He rises*)
VICTORIA. So I'm the heroine!
TOM. What do you mean?
VICTORIA (*indicating the script*) Victoria Gilchrist—your heroine. You've described her exactly like me.
TOM (*sitting on the R arm of the chair*) Really? How odd!
VICTORIA (*reading from the script*) "The scene is set in the drawing-room of Mr and Mrs Gilchrist's home in Battersea." (*She turns a page and laughs*) Ha, ha! I like that! "Opening Chorus", it says, and then a blank page.

(*The* BLACK BACKING *behind the gauze* FLIES AWAY)

TOM. I haven't written the words yet.
VICTORIA. Who sings it?
TOM. The whole company.

(*Behind the gauze the* LIGHTS *snap up to half, revealing the opening set of Tom's play.*
This is the drawing-room of Mr and Mrs Gilchrist, a late-Victorian or Edwardian couple of considerable financial standing, but the set should merely suggest this without being elaborate. Up C, *in front of a skycloth, is a high window-piece, a double door stands at an angle* R, *and a fireplace, with a section of wall over it, is* L. *There need be no wall connecting these*

features. A grand piano stands up R *between the doors and window, the keyboard up stage, angled so that the pianist will face down* C. *Above it is a piano-stool. The set is masked* R *and* L *with permanent neutral flats or velvet legs which remain unchanged throughout.*
When the LIGHTS *snap up, the* WHOLE COMPANY *are grouped on stage for the opening number. They are static and unsmiling.* TOM *and* VICTORIA *do not look round. They are sitting close in the armchair, absorbed in the script.*)

VICTORIA. What are all those people doing in our drawing-room?
TOM (*stumped for the moment*) Er . . . (*Suddenly inspired*) Singing!

(VICTORIA *laughs indulgently. She stands, places the script on the seat, and removes her coat.* TOM *rises and moves a few steps down* R)

You know, it occurs to me, it doesn't matter much *what* they sing as long as they look pretty and smile.

(*As one man the whole* COMPANY *switch on smiles, as instant as electric light bulbs*)

"TRA, LA, LA"   No. 1
FULL COMPANY

TOM (*singing*)
    Tra, la, la, la, la, la,
VICTORIA (*singing*)
    They could just sing "Tra, la, la."
(*She leaves her coat on the armchair and moves close to* Tom)
TOM.   While the audience settles
BOTH (*making it up as they go along*)
    And wonders who they are.

(VICTORIA *laughs*)

TOM.   Their dresses show it's summer,

(*The* AUTHOR'S FLAT GAUZE FLIES AWAY)

VICTORIA. And the lighting shows it's day,
BOTH (*with a gesture*)
    With so much sunlight——

(*The* LIGHTS *come up to full*)
    ——streaming their way.

(*The whole* ENSEMBLE *take up the number*)

ALL.   It's a summer noon, it's the opening tune
    And we think some words will follow soon
    But it comes to much the same
    If we only sing Tra, la, la.
    (*with descant*) Tra, la, la; Tra, la, la.
    If you'll all be kind, we believe you'll find
    It's too early in the show to mind
    Who we are or whence we came
    So we might as well Tra, la, la.

Improvising,
Harmonizing,
While you're settling in your stall
Be at ease then,
If you please then,
For you don't have to listen at all.

(Mrs GILCHRIST *and* CORA, *characters from the Author's manuscript, sing a two-part cadenza*)

Tra, la, la; Tra, la, la.

(VICTORIA *can resist no longer. She joins the ensemble and dances amongst them, modern costume or not. They do not appear to mind, or even notice*)

ALL. If we write a song as we go along
We are sure to find the rhymes are wrong
And the metre rather lame,
So we'll only sing Tra, la, la.
Tra, la, la; Tra, la, la.
Now the end's in sight and you'll be quite right
If you tell your friend the tune was bright,
But the words were all the same,
And they sounded like Tra, la, la.

Tra, la, la; Tra, la, la.

(*As the music ends, the* LIGHTS *dim out on the ensemble, and the spotlight picks up* TOM *again. In the darkness the* ENSEMBLE *drifts quietly away and* VICTORIA *returns to* TOM)

VICTORIA. Tell me about the hero.
TOM. He doesn't appear yet. He's a policeman. He doesn't meet the girl for quite a long time.
VICTORIA. Is it quite wise?
TOM. Now, Victoria!
VICTORIA (*backing* LC *in mock terror*) I was only asking. The story sort-of begins now?
TOM (*following her, a trifle huffy*) It doesn't sort-of begin; it begins.
VICTORIA. Go on then.
TOM (*crossing* C) It's a summer evening——

(*The* LIGHTS *begin to build up on the Gilchrist set*)

——in London a long time ago.

(VICTORIA *comes down to* TOM's R)

In one of the stately homes of Battersea——

(*The* 1ST STAGE-HAND *enters down* L *carrying a long low stool. He sets this* RC, *below the piano, and exits down* R. *While he is doing this the* 2ND STAGE-HAND *enters up* L *with a pedestal, which he sets up in the* L *"corner" of the room, between the window-piece and the fireplace. He exits down* L)

(*Continuing with as little pause as possible*) —a young lady is seated at the piano——
   VICTORIA. The heroine? Me?

   (TOM *nods, and* VICTORIA *moves to above the piano and sits on the piano-stool*)

   TOM. —She is playing, softly.

   (VICTORIA *poises her hands over the keyboard in the exaggerated, high-wristed attitude of the day.* TOM *crosses* R)

Her mother stands beside her——

   (MRS GILCHRIST *shoots on from up* R, *crosses behind Victoria, and stands to her* L)

—singing——

   (MRS GILCHRIST *opens her mouth wide*)

—one hand resting lightly on her daughter's shoulder——

   (*Without looking round* MRS GILCHRIST *feels out with her right hand, finds Victoria's shoulder, and rests it there.* TOM *moves up to* R *of the piano*)

—Two of the young lady's suitors——

   (*Two rich young business men enter,* TANCRED *from* R, WILBERFORCE *from* L, *each carrying a posy behind his back. They cross to meet up* C, *then smartly turn to face down stage*)

—are listening to the song——

   (TANCRED *and* WILBERFORCE, *as one, lean their heads attentively to the* R)

—in attitudes of wrapt attention——

   (TANCRED *and* WILBERFORCE *snap their heads round to face Victoria, as each produces the posy from behind his back and holds it in front of his chest*)

—one standing, one seated.——

   (*There is some disagreement over this. Both* TANCRED *and* WILBERFORCE *bend their knees in a sitting attitude, but the* 2ND STAGE-HAND *arrives from up* L *carrying only one chair. They* BOTH *stand, bend, and then stand again in unison; then try taking it in turns. Finally the* STAGE-HAND *loses patience and, when* TANCRED *next reaches the desired position, thrusts the chair underneath him, and exits down* R. WILBERFORCE *accepts his defeat and returns his attention to Victoria. While this has been going on a* DRESSER *has arrived up* R *with Victoria's period costume and has helped her into it.* VICTORIA *then resumes her pose at the piano, and the* DRESSER *exits up* R)

Alternately they gaze admiringly at the singers and exchange hostile glances with one another.—— (*He moves down* R)

(Tancred *and* Wilberforce *move their heads slickly two or three times, then come to rest gazing at* Victoria)

—The room is beautiful——

(*The* 1st Stage-hand *enters down* R *carrying a large vase in which flowers are tastefully arranged. He crosses to the pedestal up* L, *and places the vase in position*)

—and rich——

(*The* 2nd Stage-hand *enters down* R *with a strip of carpet, which he unrolls with a flourish so the end lies in front of the fireplace,* L. *He exits down* R)

—for it is a part of Mr Gilchrist's home and an expression of Mr Gilchrist's success.

(*The* 1st Stage-hand *crosses to the double doors and flings them open.* Mr Gilchrist *marches through, strides down the strip of carpet, and reaches the fireplace as* Tom *continues*)

Mr Gilchrist stands before the fireplace——

(Mr Gilchrist *turns, back to fire, and plants his feet firmly apart. The* 2nd Stage-hand *enters through the double doors* R *carrying a portrait in a frame, which he holds with its back to the audience. He crosses to just above Mr Gilchrist. The* Dresser *returns, up* R, *and changes Victoria's shoes, then exits up* R)

—He is a wholesale grocer, a magistrate and a J.P.——

(*The* 2nd Stage-hand *turns the portrait round, and we see that it shows Mr Gilchrist in the robes of a civic dignitary, looking if possible even more smug and pompous than he does in person.* Mr Gilchrist *gives the portrait a cursory glance, nods, and the* Stage-hand *hangs it on the wall over the fireplace*)

—but primarily he is a Plain Man from the North.

(*The* 2nd Stage-hand *joins the* 1st Stage-hand *by the double doors. Their duties completed, they bow and retire, closing the doors behind them*)

(*He crosses to below the piano*) Proud and unsmiling, he eyes his possessions, and his daughter, as if counting their cost and calculating at what profit they may be sold. (*He returns to his armchair, picks up the script, and sits down, edging the chair a little towards offstage* R *as he does so. He opens the script and reads from it*) "Softly, in the quiet evening, the music drifts past him."

The Lights *change. The armchair fades into the shadows and* Tom *exits. The mimed music in the drawing-room becomes a reality. As she sings* Mrs Gilchrist *quietly puts up Victoria's hair.*

Scene 2
"WHERE SHALL I FIND MY LOVE?" No. 2

MRS GILCHRIST (*singing*)
  Where shall I find my love?
  Is there some distant shore
  Where I may meet one
  Infinitely sweet one
  Love him for evermore?

(MRS GILCHRIST *turns the page for* VICTORIA. TANCRED *and* WILBERFORCE *sniff the posies they carry*)

  When will my longing heart
  Sing with the lark above?
  When shall I ever
  Know it's now or never?

(MR GILCHRIST *gives a thumbs-up signal*)

  Where shall I find my love?

(TANCRED *rises*)

TANCRED (*singing*)
  I searched for her in the forest
WILBERFORCE (*singing*)
  I searched for her in the wood
MR GILCHRIST (*singing*)
  But now I greatly fear me
MRS GILCHRIST. That she has gone for good.
TANCRED. Is she drowned in some sad fountain?
WILBERFORCE. Or buried beneath a mountain?

(MR GILCHRIST *crosses up stage to between* TANCRED *and* WILBERFORCE)

TANCRED. Is she on sea?
WILBERFORCE.   Is she on land?
MR GILCHRIST. Did she get lost in the desert sand?
MRS GILCHRIST. My angel——

(TANCRED, MR GILCHRIST *and* WILBERFORCE *cross* R. MRS GILCHRIST *again turns the page for* VICTORIA)

    —don't you understand?
WILBERFORCE. That I am waiting?
TANCRED.   Palpitating?

(TANCRED *takes up position to* VICTORIA'*s* R, MR GILCHRIST *is next to* MRS GILCHRIST, *on her* L, *with* WILBERFORCE *to his* L)

ALL.   Where shall I find my love?

(MRS GILCHRIST *arranges an Alice-band on* VICTORIA, *and puts the chain of a locket around her neck*)

Is there some distant shore
Where I may meet one
Infinitely sweet one
Love him for evermore?

(MR GILCHRIST *catches* WILBERFORCE *making eyes at* VICTORIA. MR GILCHRIST *is displeased,* WILBERFORCE *dismayed, and* VICTORIA *disinterested*)

When will my longing heart
Sing with the lark above?
When shall I ever
Know it's now or never?
Where shall I find my love?

WILBERFORCE (*crossing to* L *of Mrs Gilchrist*) Thank you, Mrs Gilchrist.

TANCRED. Thank *you*, Miss Gilchrist.

WILBERFORCE. The accompaniment was beautiful!

(MRS GILCHRIST, *a little put out, glares at Wilberforce*)

TANCRED. Miss Gilchrist, there are no words.

WILBERFORCE. We are dumb with admiration.

MR GILCHRIST. And now, gentlemen, if you will step into the next room—— (*He crosses to the* L *end of the long stool,* RC)

MRS GILCHRIST. —and take some refreshment? (*She crosses* L *and exits*)

TANCRED
WILBERFORCE } (*together*) Ah, thank you.

(WILBERFORCE *breaks* L *a little,* TANCRED *crosses to* R *of Wilberforce*)

After you, Miss Gilchrist.

MR GILCHRIST (*signalling to Victoria to stay*) No, gentlemen. After you.

(WILBERFORCE *invites Tancred to lead the way. As* TANCRED *crosses,* WILBERFORCE *trips him, then turns to grin smugly at Victoria. He starts to exit without looking where he is going, giving* TANCRED *the chance to trip him in return. They exit* L)

You will accept one of these gentlemen tonight!

VICTORIA. Papa! I . . .

MR GILCHRIST (*crossing to below the fireplace*) Now don't interrupt me, Victoria! For over a year now, they've been coming here, drinking my Madeira till I've scarcely a drop in the cellar. You'll accept one of them now, tonight, and put them out of their misery and my house.

VICTORIA. But, Papa, I don't know why you favour them so.

MR GILCHRIST. They're good men. They've made a success. They travel first class. Their two shops are patronized by the gentry. D'you sneer at shops?

VICTORIA (*rising*) No, Papa, I . . .

MR GILCHRIST (*lyrically*) Their turnover must run into millions.

(VICTORIA *crosses to* R *of Mr Gilchrist*)

VICTORIA. You want me to marry for money, Papa?
MR GILCHRIST. Why not? Your mother did.
VICTORIA. Did any good come of it?
MR GILCHRIST. Well, I look at you and wonder.

(VICTORIA *crosses and sits on the long stool, below the piano*)

But she's never complained and she always travels first class. I'm a magistrate and a J.P., I've made my mark in Battersea. (*He crosses to the piano and leans on it*) We're entering the age of the Business Men. They're taking over, the future! And you'll oblige me by not being left behind. (*He crosses up* L) I shall now send the gentlemen in to you.

(VICTORIA *rises and crosses to* C)

VICTORIA. Papa!
MR GILCHRIST. One at a time, of course.
VICTORIA. But, Papa!
MR GILCHRIST. You have my commands—obey them. (*He exits* L)

(VICTORIA *crosses down* C)

VICTORIA. Oh, how can I choose between them? You couldn't put a pin between them! If I married one, I would think myself a bigamist! Here they come! Whatever shall I do?

(VICTORIA *hurriedly crosses and sits below the piano as* TANCRED *enters from up* L, *carrying his posy behind him. He crosses to* C)

TANCRED. Oo-oo! May I come in?
VICTORIA (*wincing*) Come in, Mr Wilberforce.
TANCRED. Tancred.
VICTORIA. I beg your pardon.
TANCRED (*crossing to* L *of Victoria*) Miss Gilchrist, I have your father's permission to speak. (*He kneels and offers the posy*) I am here to lay all I have at your feet.
VICTORIA (*accepting and examining the rather small posy*) All you have?
TANCRED (*rising; joyously*) Oh, I'm so proud of it! Last year . . . (*he feels that Victoria is not really paying attention so he takes away the posy and puts it on the seat beside her*) last year, out of my beautiful shop, I made over a million pounds!
VICTORIA. Oh.
TANCRED. Miss Gilchrist, Victoria, (*he goes to sit beside her, realizes in the nick of time that the posy is there, and snatches it up before lowering his weight*) may I tell you the secret of my heart? It's a trade secret. (*He hands the posy back to Victoria*)
VICTORIA (*bleakly*) I am honoured, sir.
TANCRED. Tomorrow I am going to take over *Mr Wilberforce's* beautiful shop.
VICTORIA (*puzzled*) Take it over?

TANCRED. I've bought up all the shares. (*Gleefully*) He little knows! Tomorrow Wilberforce's will be *mine!*
VICTORIA. Poor Mr Wilberforce!
TANCRED (*gravely*) This is business, Miss Gilchrist. Let the best man win!
VICTORIA. By all means. But it's puzzling, sir. If you have made a million pounds, why do you want another shop?
TANCRED. To make another million.
VICTORIA. But why . . . ?
TANCRED (*rising, excitedly*) To buy another shop to make another million (*he moves round* L *to* C) to buy another shop to make another million to buy another shop to make another million (*his excitement has started him dancing*) to buy another shop to . . .
VICTORIA. Sir! (*She claps her hands and calls louder*) Please!

(TANCRED, *breathless and a little giddy, stops dancing*)

TANCRED. Thank you. I was dazzled by my vision of the future. (*He crosses to* L *of Victoria*) Victoria, will you share it with me?

(VICTORIA *hands him back his posy, rises and moves to the* R *end of the long stool*)

VICTORIA. I cannot, sir.
TANCRED (*rising and then kneeling on the stool*) Victoria! I love you. Will you marry me?
VICTORIA. No, sir.
TANCRED. Good heavens! Are you confusing me with someone else?
VICTORIA. No, sir.
TANCRED (*standing on the stool*) Ah, I begin to see daylight! You love another.
VICTORIA. No.
TANCRED. My friend Wilberforce!
VICTORIA. No! No!
TANCRED. Yes! Yes! (*Pointing* L *so violently he almost loses his balance*) When I entered the room you called me by his name. You love him!
VICTORIA (*losing her temper and tipping up the* R *end of the seat*) No!

(TANCRED *falls off, down* C)

TANCRED. Yes!
VICTORIA. Oh, very well, then, yes! *Yes!*
TANCRED (*suddenly the heartbroken good loser*) Then, Miss Gilchrist, I have no more to say. I will be the first to congratulate him. (*He gives the posy back to Victoria*) Good-bye. (*He moves up to below the chair up* C, *facing up stage*)

(WILBERFORCE *enters down* L, *crosses up to beside Tancred and smirks at him, then gazes out of the window.* TANCRED *turns, sees that Wilberforce is still holding his posy behind his back. Gently he removes all the flowers, then exits* L)

VICTORIA. Oh, what have I done? I shall never forgive myself. And here comes the other. (*She sits on the long stool*)

(WILBERFORCE *turns to her*)

WILBERFORCE. May I come in?
VICTORIA. Yes, sir.
WILBERFORCE. Oh, Miss Gilchrist, I'm a happy man today! I must tell you the reason or bust! (*Realizing this is not a word to use in the presence of a lady*) I beg your pardon! Last year I made a million out of my beautiful store—(*he turns to face* L, *unwittingly revealing to Victoria the empty posy he carries behind him*) and tomorrow I take over Mr Tancred's beautiful store. (*Beside himself with excitement*) He doesn't know it yet. . . .

(VICTORIA *cannot help bursting into laughter.* TANCRED *turns and sits beside her*)

Oh you're *sharing* my happiness. (*He is emboldened to put an arm around her shoulder*) Oh, Victoria, I have two beautiful big stores! Marry me and we'll have a lot of little ones!
VICTORIA. Sir . . .
WILBERFORCE. Stores, I mean.
VICTORIA (*rising and moving to* R *of the seat*) I cannot, sir.
WILBERFORCE. What?
VICTORIA. I cannot marry you.
WILBERFORCE (*turning and kneeling his* R *knee on the seat*) But, Victoria, I love you. (*With a dramatic movement he produces the posy from behind his back. The effect would have been improved if the posy had still contained a few blooms. He begins a desperate search for his lost flowers*)

(VICTORIA *helps in the search and they finish together searching under the long stool. It is then that* WILBERFORCE *notices she is still carrying Tancred's flowers*)

(*Standing*) This can only mean you love another.
VICTORIA (*standing*) No!
WILBERFORCE. Yes! My friend Tancred!
VICTORIA. No!
WILBERFORCE (*breaking to* L *of the seat*) Yes, yes! You love *him!*
VICTORIA. Very well, then. Yes, *yes!*
WILBERFORCE (*crossing down* C) Then I have no more to say. Forgive my importunity.
VICTORIA. Oh, no, dear Mr Wilberforce, forgive *me!* (*She hands Tancred's posy to* WILBERFORCE *who is too dazed to refuse. Dramatically, she backs to* R *as she apologizes*) Forgive me! Forgive me! Forgive me! (*Turning to the audience, conversationally*) Forgive me. (*She exits quickly,* R)

(WILBERFORCE *crosses tragically to the piano and puts down the posy*)

WILBERFORCE. I will rejoice in my friend's joy. I will be the first to congratulate him.

(TANCRED *enters* L *and* WILBERFORCE *turns towards him. They approach each other swiftly, with outstretched hands, and, typically, both think of exactly the same things to say*)

B

TANCRED
WILBERFORCE
{ *(together)* Congratulations, old man! (*They shake hands*) What do you mean? ... You are to marry Miss Gilchrist. (*They drop the handshake*) What? ... (*Stepping back a pace each*) She told me she loved you. ... What are you saying? You are mocking me, sir. ... Not I, sir. ... Then (*each with a stamp of the foot*) stop saying everything I say! ... (*In exasperation*) Do you hear me? ... (*Both put their hands on their hips, truculently*) She told me ... (*Both think this has gone on long enough. They relax and try a more reasoning tone. Unfortunately they both try it at the same moment*) She told .. (*A pause*) She ... (*They turn away from each other, whistle a few bars, then turn back to spit it out in a rush—still together*) She told me *you* were the lucky man. (*They both face front*) This is beyond bearing. (*Facing each other again*) Damn you, sir. (*Getting more and more angry*) Dolt! Idiot! Madman! Lunatic!

(*They fly at each other's throats and fight furiously. When the battle is interrupted by* MR GILCHRIST, *who enters* L, WILBERFORCE *is on Tancred's* L)

MR GILCHRIST. Gentlemen! (*He crosses to between them and separates them*) This unseemly wrangle! Part I say! What is your quarrel?
TANCRED
WILBERFORCE } (*together, as before*) Your daughter told ...
MR GILCHRIST. One at a time, gentlemen!
TANCRED
WILBERFORCE } (*inseparable*) Your daughter told me ...
MR GILCHRIST. One at a time, gentlemen, please! (*Pointing to Wilbeforce*) Now, sir.
WILBERFORCE. Your daughter told me she loved Mr Tancred.
MR GILCHRIST. Is that an excuse for flying at his throat?
TANCRED. But, sir—your daughter told me she loved Mr Wilberforce.
MR GILCHRIST. Is that an excuse for flying—*what?*
TANCRED
WILBERFORCE } (*together*) Yes, sir.
MR GILCHRIST. And accepted you both?
TANCRED
WILBERFORCE } (*together*) Yes, sir.
MR GILCHRIST (*raging; breaking down* R) I will never forgive her. I will turn her out of the house!

(MRS GILCHRIST *carrying a note, enters* L, *distracted. She crosses to* LC)

MRS GILCHRIST. I will never forgive you! You have turned her out of the house.
THE THREE MEN (*together*) What? Who?

Mrs Gilchrist (*crossing to* L *of Wilberforce*) Our daughter. She has run away!
The Three Men (*together*) Run away?
Mrs Gilchrist. She left a note on her pincushion.
The Three Men (*together*) Her pincushion?
Tancred. Her pincushion!
Wilberforce. That's bad!
Mrs Gilchrist (*reading the note*) "Dear Mama. Have run away. Forgive Papa. Love, Victoria."

(*The* Men *are horror-stricken.* Wilberforce *crosses to* L *of Mrs Gilchrist.* Mr Gilchrist *moves up to the piano and, rather surprisingly, finds a pistol under the lid*)

Mr Gilchrist. I have done this! Grief and shame will conspire to destroy me. (*He crosses* C, *brandishing the pistol*)

(Mrs Gilchrist, *noting his intention, hurries to his* L *and kneels to implore her husband to spare himself*)

I am not worthy to live! (*He points the pistol at his temple*)
Tancred. No, no!
Wilberforce. Spare yourself!
Mrs Gilchrist. For my sake!
Tancred. Sir, we will find her.
Wilberforce. We will bring her safely home.
Mr Gilchrist (*rather relieved to be able to relent*) You will really pursue her?
Tancred. More than that; we will catch her.
Mr Gilchrist (*lowering the pistol*) Gentleman, you are generous. And I hereby swear that whichever of you first lays hands on her shall be her husband.

(Mrs Gilchrist *rises*)

Tancred. You mean that, sir?
Mr Gilchrist. I swear it.
Wilberforce. Let us start immediately.
Tancred (*crossing* R *towards the double doors*) Let us not waste a moment! (*He opens the doors*)
Wilberforce. I say, Tancred!
Tancred. What is it?
Wilberforce. You must start fair.
Tancred. Sorry. I got carried away.

(*Together,* Tancred *and* Wilberforce *cross down* L *and crouch "on their marks" as for the start of a sprint.* Mr *and* Mrs Gilchrist *move up* C)

Mr Gilchrist (*in the voice of an athletics match starter*) Are you ready? (*He raises the pistol*) Set?

(Wilberforce *and* Tancred *tense forward*)

(*He fires the gun*)

(WILBERFORCE *and* TANCRED *prance off* R *with a high-stepping action, at a steady trot*)

I must go too, Biddy. (*He hands the pistol to* MRS GILCHRIST)
MRS GILCHRIST. Oh, Husband!
MR GILCHRIST. I must assist them. Our daughter alone in this great city! And night will fall in a few hours. (*He crosses down* L) I must go too.
MRS GILCHRIST. And what must I do?
MR GILCHRIST. Women must weep.

(MRS GILCHRIST *weeps*)

(*He crouches "on his mark", then straightens*) Keep a lamp in the . . . (*He crouches, straightens*) Keep the home fires . . . (*He crouches, straightens*) Wish me success. (*He crouches*) Good-bye, Biddy.
MRS GILCHRIST (*raising the pistol*) Good-bye, Oscar. (*She fires the pistol*)

(MR GILCHRIST *trots off* R. MRS GILCHRIST *sinks weeping on the piano. The* LIGHTS *dim to half. The* 1ST STAGE-HAND *enters* L, *picks up the long stool below the piano and is about to take it off* L, *when he realizes* MRS GILCHRIST *is still draped over the piano. He puts down the stool, crosses to her and taps her on the shoulder.* MRS GILCHRIST *looks up, sees who it is and stops weeping. She shrugs, and exits* R. *The* STAGE-HAND *returns to pick up the stool as the* LIGHTS *dim to* BLACK-OUT *and—*

the RUNNING TABS *close*

"CHASE MUSIC" No. 3

SCENE 3

The scene is played in front of RUNNING TABS *which depict Streets of London.*

When the LIGHTS *come up,* TOM *enters* R *and stands extreme* R. *As he continues his narrative,* VICTORIA *enters* R *and crosses behind him. She trots across the stage, suiting her actions to Tom's description.*

TOM. At first Victoria ran distractedly. She tore along without sense of direction. She hardly saw where she was. At every street corner, a pitiful figure, she wrung her hands, wondering which road to take. It hardly seemed to matter, for she knew she had nowhere to go.

(VICTORIA *exits* L. TANCRED *and* WILBERFORCE, *still prancing, enter* R, *cross behind Tom and do a high-stepping mark time, just* L *of Tom*)

Tancred and Wilberforce were as yet far behind. They had not sighted her. Indeed, each was so afraid that the other would find her first, that they dared not lose sight of one another.

SCENE 4 FOLLOW THAT GIRL

(*Smartly*, TANCRED *and* WILBERFORCE *turn their heads to face each other and then, running perfectly abreast, they continue across the stage and exit* L. MR GILCHRIST *enters* R *and begins to cross. He suits his actions to Tom's description*)

As for poor Mr Gilchrist, he set out bravely enough, but his emotion so interfered with his breathing that he was very soon scarcely able to run at all. He ran into lamp-posts, he tripped over kerbs, and, weeping, ran on again, lifting his streaming eyes to the evening sky.

MR GILCHRIST *exits* L.

SCENE 4

The RUNNING TABS *open to reveal Battersea Park. This is suggested by a floral ground-row set against the skycloth, a cut-out bush here and there; perhaps even a tree, but nothing too realistic. Down* L *is a small, grass-covered mound, just big enough for Cora to pose on, rather uncomfortably. By it is a stuffed dove and a cornucopia.*

When the CURTAINS *part* WALTER MISKIN *is painting a picture, the canvas standing on an easel set well up* RC. *He has chosen Battersea Park as his locale to give extra realism to his new work of art which is to be called "Leonora and the Dove".* WALTER *is rapt and enchanted with himself.*

TOM (*continuing*) Near at hand, in Battersea Park, an artist stood painting in the sunlight. He was Walter Miskin, R.A.—successful enough, but incorrigibly Bohemian. Painting was his passion——

(WALTER *paints passionately*)

——and he had but one hobby.

(WALTER *reaches for his hip-flask, takes a quick swig, and puts it back in his pocket*)

His wife Cora was a simple soul——

(CORA *enters* R, *dressed in Pre-Raphaelite costume*)

——and a strong supporter of the Pre-Raphaelite movement.

(CORA *droops*)

He had married her to save the cost of a model——

(CORA *moves to* LC, *then turns up to face Walter*)

——but during the years a great love had grown between them.

(CORA *and* WALTER *blow kisses to each other, beaming with pleasure*)

The title of the current masterpiece was to be "Leonora and the Dove".

(CORA *crosses to the grassy mound and takes up her pose*)

"I'M AWAY"   No. 4

(*Tom crosses to Cora, hands her the cornucopia, perches the stuffed dove on the other hand and arranges her dress.* CORA *is very uncomfortable, but amused and acquiescent. When he has finished,* TOM *returns to down* R)

Miskin was in great form that day, but Cora was a little restless. (*He exits down* R)

 (CORA *yawns and fidgets*)

WALTER (*singing*)
  Be still, my dearest Cora,
  Be still, my dearest love,
  (*He crosses to Cora and re-positions the dove*)
  For now you're Leonora,
  Complete with turtle dove.
  (*Satisfied, he returns to the easel*)

CORA (*singing*)
  But who is Leonora?

WALTER. I'm not exactly sure,
  But people will adore her
  Because she is——
  (*He plonks some paint on the canvas*)
    —so pure.
  (*He crosses down* C, *looking at Cora*)

CORA. But if I'm Leonora
  I'd rather like to know
  These Fauna and these Flora—
  Are they just for show?

WALTER (*crossing to her*)
  Be quiet, my dearest Cora.
  I know you must be tired
  But now you're Leonora
  (*He rearranges the position of her hand*)
  And I—I'm inspired!
  (*He returns to the easel and paints with a flourish as he sings*)

  When the sun is bright
  The light is right
  And I'm well stocked with Chinese white
  I can safely say
  "I'm away!"

CORA (*setting down the cornucopia and dove*)
  And he's got the urge
  He's on the verge
  (*Crossing to* R *of Walter*)
  Of making all the colours merge
  In a bold display

WALTER } (together) { I'm away!
CORA   { He's away!

(*A group of* BYSTANDERS *begins to gather. They gaze with interest at the artist and his model and, particularly, at the partly-finished canvas*)

WALTER. How's the hair?
Rich and rare!
And oh those bones!
The fleshly tones
Will propagate a complex in Burne Jones
CORA. It may not sell
WALTER. But what the hell?
I've got my blessed Damozel
CORA. And a lovely day
WALTER. I'm away!

(WALTER, *aware of the interested spectators—customers possibly?—puts the easel a little further down stage so that they can admire it better*)

CORA. I'm stiff and sore
And I'm longing for
My tea.
WALTER. We'll stop at half-past three
CORA. You just don't care
And your wife must bear
The brunt
You're worse than Holman Hunt
WALTER. But keep still, dear,
Please if you will, dear,
You may catch a nasty chill, dear,
But bear with me, I pray
Because today's a day
When I can safely say
"I'm away!"
CORA. He's away.
BYSTANDERS. He's away, he's away.

(*The* BYSTANDERS *dance, and* CORA *joins them*)

He's the hearty type
Of arty type
The naughty Chelsea party type
WALTER. Boop-a-doop! Ole!
ALL. He's away!
CORA. When he hops about
And starts to shout
I know there's not a shred of doubt
That the work's O.K.
ALL. He's away!

       See that bird!
       Oh, my word!
       It does look real
       It makes you feel
       You'd like to take it home
       For your evening meal
       And we just can't wait
       Until the date
       It's reproduced in copper plate
       On a pink tea-tray
WALTER (*furiously*)
       Go away!
ALL.   He's away!
       He's away!

(*After applause at the end of the number, the music begins again and the* BYSTANDERS *exit.* CORA *returns to sit on the mound, fanning herself with the dove.* WALTER *goes back to the easel, singing lightly and gaily, half dancing. He puts his palette and brush in his bag, takes a quick drink from his hip-flask which he then places on the ground,* LC, *leaning it against the mound. He returns to the easel as the music finishes*)

 CORA (*with sudden vehemence*) Walter! There's something we've forgotten!
 WALTER (*gaily absorbed*) What again?
 CORA (*melodramatically*) We've forgotten about our lost child!
 WALTER. Of course! I must remember I'm in the grip of a Great Sorrow! (*He droops suitably*)
 CORA (*rising and crossing up* C *to Walter*) While the crowd was here we ought to have displayed his portrait.
 WALTER. You're right, my dear. How else can we hope to find him? (*He takes "Leonora and the Dove" off the easel and parks the canvas behind the mound, then brings the empty easel down* C *and turns it to face the audience. He stands to* L *of it*)
 CORA. Let us display it now! (*She reaches behind the mound and produces another large canvas*) It's a very good likeness! Someone may recognize him. (*She crosses to* R *of the easel and displays the canvas. It is a portrait of a baby, extravagantly dressed*)
 WALTER. Yes, some passer-by may stop and say: "Haven't I seen that face somewhere before?"
 CORA (*crossing in front of the easel to Walter, and kissing him*) Oh, what a day that will be!

(TANCRED *and* WILBERFORCE *enter* L, *still trotting neck and neck as they were when we last saw them,* WILBERFORCE *on the* R, TANCRED *to his* L)

 WALTER. Here's someone now!

(CORA *and* WALTER *watch in breathless excitement as* TANCRED *and* WILBERFORCE *prance across to down* R. *As they reach the exit they do a*

SCENE 4 FOLLOW THAT GIRL 19

double take, and swing round together, having seen the baby portrait from the corner of their eyes. The MISKINS *watch intently*)

TANCRED. Did you see that picture?
WILBERFORCE (*excitedly*) The very thing!
TANCRED. But if we stop we shall lose track of Victoria!
WILBERFORCE. Business before pleasure, old boy.
TANCRED. You're right, old man.

(*They approach the Miskins and take off their hats*)

WILBERFORCE. Sir, this picture . . .
CORA. You recognize him?
WALTER. Our lost child?
CORA. You know where he is? Take us to him!
TANCRED. Never seen him in my life, ma'am, but we wish to purchase this picture.
WALTER (*sadly turning away*) It is not for sale.

(CORA *turns sadly up stage, resting her* L *hand on the picture.* WALTER *comes a pace down stage, facing front*)

WILBERFORCE. We offer you a thousand pounds.
TANCRED (*crossing down* R) A thousand and one.
WALTER (*forcefully*) It is not for sale!
WILBERFORCE. A thousand and two.
TANCRED. A thousand and fifty.
WILBERFORCE. Eleven hundred.
TANCRED. Twelve hundred.

(CORA *turns and advances on them with terrible magnificence*)

CORA. Are you Americans, gentlemen, that you don't understand the language? It is not for sale. (*She turns and crosses to* R *of Walter*)
WILBERFORCE (*crossing to* R *of the picture*) Oh, but that baby's face!
TANCRED. That sensitive skin!
WILBERFORCE. That lovely complexion!
TANCRED. That beauty.
WALTER (*flattered*) You are great connoisseurs of art, sirs.
WILBERFORCE. Connoisseurs? No, sir! We're business men.
TANCRED. And we're looking for a soap advertisement.
WILBERFORCE. Yes, that's right.

(CORA *and* WALTER *advance angrily on Tancred and Wilberforce, speaking together*)

CORA ⎫
          ⎬ (*together*) ⎧ Soap advertisement? Out of my sight, you twin barbarians. You trifling nincompoops! Begone!
WALTER ⎭   ⎨ Vandals! Goths! Soap advertisement! Be off! Be off!

(TANCRED *and* WILBERFORCE *are forced off stage,* R, CORA *and* WALTER *following them. At once* TANCRED *and* WILBERFORCE *re-enter*, *up* R, *steal the picture and easel, and hurry off with them, up* L. *The* MISKINS *reappear up* R *and start to give chase*)

MISKINS. Stop! Stop! Stop, thief! Stop! Stop!

(*They exit up* L, *but after a moment* WALTER *re-enters and collects his hip-flask from the mound before resuming the chase.* TOM *enters up* R *and walks down* C. *Although he is now dressed as a policeman, he still carries his script*)

TOM (*reading from the script*) "And so another chase began. While Mr Gilchrist ran, seeking his child, Mr and Mrs Miskin sought the likeness of theirs. (*He crosses to* LC, *removes his helmet and places it on the mound. Then he returns to* C *stage*) Meanwhile Constable Blenkinsop wandered on his lonely beat through Battersea Park. He was not to catch sight of Victoria for several long hours——

(VICTORIA *enters* R, *runs determinedly across the stage and exits* L)

"FOLLOW THAT GIRL" No. 5

(*His eyes follow her. He looks back at the script. He is about to call after her, but changes his mind. Instead he produces a pencil and makes a note in the script. He resumes reading*) —Tom Blenkinsop, on his lonely beat in Battersea Park, caught sight of Victoria for the first time, and afterwards loved her for ever."

TOM (*singing*) That girl!
That girl!
Enter a wonderful girl!
And now all I can see
Is a cloud of dust
But that girl must
Belong to me!

Follow that girl
I'll have to
Follow that girl
That girl who
Came into my life
From nowhere
Now I'll have to go where-
Ever she goes
I'll have to
Follow my nose
Until the
Day she is my wife
I'll follow that girl.

I never
Knew a man could fall in love
So suddenly

But when she
Ran away the only thought
That came to me
Was, I must
(*Moving downstage a little*)

Follow that girl
I've got to
Follow that girl
That girl is
Definitely worth
My ardour
If she runs I'll run the harder
Right across the earth
I'll follow that girl.
(*He crosses down* R)

Here is a case
Of love at first sight
Making me burst right
Out of my daily routine
Where is that face
I saw so briefly?
What was it chiefly
Made it the face of a queen?
How can I trace
The eyes, the hair, the lips
I hardly had time to see?
(*He crosses down* C)
Is this the face
That launched a thousand ships?
No, but it's launching me.
(*Crossing down* L)
And I must

Follow that girl
I'll have to
Follow that girl
That girl who
Came into my life
From nowhere
Now I'll have to go where-
Ever she goes
I'll have to
Follow my nose
Until the
Day she is my wife
I'll follow that girl.
(*He moves up* C)

I never
Knew a man could fall in love
So suddenly
But when she
Ran away the only thought
That came to me
Was, I must
(*Crossing down* R)

Follow that girl
I've got to
Follow that girl
That girl is
(*Crossing down* L)
Definitely worth
My ardour
If she runs I'll run the harder
Right across the earth
I'll follow that girl.

(*When the music finishes,* TOM *collects his helmet and stands* LC. WALTER *enters up* L *and crosses to* R. *He carries a large* WANTED *poster and is looking for a tree to hammer it to. If there isn't one, he affixes it to one of the neutral flats*)

WALTER. Evening, Constable.
TOM. Good evening, sir.
WALTER (*hammering*) I've made great progress while you've been singing here. I've drawn portraits of the thieves and done several two-minute sketches for circulation. (*He hammers again*)
TOM (*crossing* C) Thieves, sir?
WALTER. The men who stole my picture. Weren't you here? No, no, of course not, or they would scarcely have proceeded. Ha, ha! Well, there they are! (*He adds another touch to the poster, then crosses to* R *of* TOM) Hadn't you better be after them?
TOM. I'm on my beat, sir.
WALTER. Oh, come now!
TOM. I've had my orders.
WALTER. But there's a hundred pounds reward!
TOM. Then I'll do my best.
WALTER. Splendid! Splen . . . (*He stops abruptly and takes a step back, staring, riveted, at Tom's face*)
TOM. Something wrong, sir?
WALTER. You have a very strong look of my Cousin Herbert—he's been dead for years. (*He stares for another tense moment*) Well, look alive, young man. Better have some reproductions. (*He produces a sketch-pad and pencil and sketches rapidly*) Take a lot! Take two! (*He hands the first two sketches to Tom, then goes on sketching*)

(*A* GENTLEMAN *passes by, entering from down* R *and going off* L)

SCENE 4   FOLLOW THAT GIRL   23

(*Diving at the passer-by*) Two-minute sketches. A hundred pounds reward!
  TOM (*examining his sketches*) They look remarkably alike.
  WALTER. No. What? (*He crosses to* L *of* TOM) I've given you two of the same one! Snap! Ha, ha! (*He hurriedly gives him another sketch*)

  (*A* 2ND GENTLEMAN *crosses from up* R *and exits up* L)

  (*Dashing up to the new arrival*) Two-minute sketches! All my own work!

  (MR GILCHRIST *jogs on up* L *and crosses down* R)

(*Following Mr Gilchrist*) Two-minute sketches . . .
  MR GILCHRIST. Too long.
  WALTER. A hundred pounds reward . . .
  MR GILCHRIST. Too much. Oh, Constable, I need your help.
  WALTER. Have you lost your child, too?
  MR GILCHRIST. How did you know?
  WALTER (*staring at Tom again*) Extraordinary! My dead Cousin Herbert to the life!

  (*A* GIRL *enters down* R *and crosses to exit down* L)

(*Dashing after the Girl*) Two-minute sketches! Wanted! Wanted! (*He exits after the Girl down* L)
  MR GILCHRIST (*tapping his head*) Wanting!

  (TOM *crosses towards Mr Gilchrist but he, intent on following Walter's progress, crosses Tom and finishes on Tom's* L)

(*Producing a photograph from his wallet*) Look, here's my missing daughter's photograph—oh dear, no, that's not her; that's my wife taking the waters at Bath. (*He tries his wallet again;* TOM *crosses to* L *of Mr Gilchrist who finds some more photographs but, for a moment can't find Tom. When he realizes Tom is now on his left, he resumes shuffling through his snapshots*) That's just the waters: that's just Bath: that's just a bath; leaking slightly! (*He laughs gayly, but catching* TOM'S *serious, "patient" expression, stops abruptly with a little cough, and continues*) That's me: me again: me on a bear-skin rug: me bare on a skin rug: me skinning a bear on a rug: that's my daughter's two suitors.

  (TOM *produces the two-minute sketches*)

Oh, I see you already have pictures of them. (*The truth dawns*) What? Why? (*He turns to examine the wanted poster on the tree*) What! *Wanted? No!*
  TOM. Yes!
  MR GILCHRIST. *Yes!* They're criminals, and they're chasing my daughter! (*He rushes up* L *and shouts off*) Help! Police! (*He runs down* L) Police! (*He notices the still-patient Tom and crosses to him*) Oh, of course, you're here! You've got to catch these men. My daughter's at their mercy!
  TOM. Come now, keep calm, sir. You know these men?
  MR GILCHRIST. Haven't I told you?

TOM. Then you can help us to identify them. Come along!
They run off down R *together as—*
the RUNNING TABS *close*

SCENE 5

The scene is Streets of London.

"CHASE MUSIC" No. 6

When the music has been playing for a short while TOM *re-enters down* R.

TOM. Meanwhile, Victoria had ceased to look about her and ran doggedly forward.

(VICTORIA *enters down* R *and begins to cross, as before*)

She had made her way south as far as Battersea Park. Her breath came shorter; her legs ached horribly. She left the park at the West Gate and laboured towards Albert Bridge.

(VICTORIA *exits down* L. TANCRED *and* WILBERFORCE *enter down* R)

Toiling after her came Tancred and Wilberforce, carrying their picture. Perhaps they had sighted her, for they no longer watched one another warily, but peered eagerly forward as if their quarry were almost theirs.

(TANCRED *and* WILBERFORCE *cross, their hands shading their eyes. They exit down* L)

Travelling after them, by some strange coincidence, for he had not yet set eyes on them, came Constable Blenkinsop. He did not run—no policeman ever runs—he covered the ground easily with long, purposeful strides. (*Suiting his action to his words, he crosses to* L *stage*) His calm walk had easily outstripped Mr Gilchrist's agitated run——

(MR GILCHRIST *enters down* R, *breathless and tottering, and stumbles his way to* C *stage, where he pauses for breath*)

—and now, to his shame, Mr Gilchrist was suddenly overtaken by his wife——

(MRS GILCHRIST *enters down* R *and, covering the ground in a few enormous strides, crosses* C *to Mr Gilchrist, and clings to him*)

—who had been unable to bear the suspense alone. Impervious to her tears, he ordered her peremptorily home, and—knowing she was watching—strode like a hero in the direction of Albert Bridge.

MR GILCHRIST *braces himself and strides off down* L. MRS GILCHRIST *miserably watches him go before turning sadly in her tracks and making for the exit down* R. *As she does so,* CORA *and* WALTER *enter down* R.

Scene 6

They cross Mrs Gilchrist RC *and continue across the stage to exit down* L. MRS GILCHRIST *exits down* R. TOM *follows Cora and Walter off down* L *as—*

the RUNNING TABS *open*

SCENE 6

The scene is Albert Bridge. Rostrums run from L *to* R, *set well up stage, masked by groundrows painted to represent the parapets of the bridge. A cut-out representation of the bridge's own peculiar suspension system can be at* R *of* C *there are steps up to the top of the parapet, for the convenience of intending suicides. On the upstage side there is a ramp down which Victoria will appear to "float" gently later in the scene. The maximum amount of stage-space possible should remain down stage of the rostrums.*

When the RUNNING TABS *open,* VICTORIA *runs on* L. *For a moment she leans against the parapet, gasping for breath. In despair, she then climbs the steps and is poised as if to jump when* WALTER *and* CORA *run on, down* L. WALTER *carries an easel and his bag of painter's equipment. They see Victoria and call out to her.*

"SOLITARY STRANGER"   No. 7

CORA. Stop!
WALTER. Cease!
CORA.   Don't go in!
        (*Singing*) You look so lovely standing there
        With river breezes in your hair
        Before you jump with ill-advised temerity
        Allow my husband to preserve you
        For posterity.

(VICTORIA *relents, climbs down and sits on the bottom step*)

WALTER. Take her up tenderly
        Lift her with care.

(CORA *and* WALTER *cross to Victoria, lift her up to stand on the parapet and "pose" her in an attitude of Edwardian despair; right hand to forehead, left arm stretched out appealingly.* WALTER *rapidly sets up his easel and begins to paint*)

CORA (*crossing down* LC)
        Oh, Walter, here's the masterpiece
        Your public now expects
        A tragical disaster piece
        Called—
WALTER. "Suicide Reflects"

CORA. Oh no, that's too obtrusive, dear,
It's better to display
A title more elusive, dear,
Like—
WALTER. "Emily at Bay"
(*He crosses to* L *of Victoria and re-poses her right hand*)
CORA. But say her name's not Emily
   (WALTER *crosses to* R *of Cora*)
We wouldn't want to change her
We need a title
Obscure, yet vital—
Like— (*inspired*)
"SOLITARY STRANGER!"
(*She crosses to Victoria's* L)
WALTER (*spoken*) Yes!
(*He returns to the easel and works with a will*)
CORA. Solitary Stranger,
Where did you come from?
What have you run from?
Did you do something wrong?
(*She offers Victoria a helping hand.* VICTORIA *moves down the steps and comes down* RC, CORA *to her* L)
Can you be in danger?
Let us befriend you
Couldn't we send you
Back to where you belong?

D'you seek a lonely street
For cover?
Or have you flown to meet
Your lover?
(VICTORIA *crosses to* L *of Cora*)
Solitary Stranger,
Are you in hiding?
Are you deciding
Here you will spend your days
And be a solitary stranger
Always.
(VICTORIA, *in a rush, returns to the top of the parapet as a group of* BYSTANDERS *enter.* CORA *follows Victoria and just manages to stop her from jumping*)
1ST GENTLEMAN BYSTANDER.
Isn't it a pity.
2ND GENTLEMAN BYSTANDER.
She's very pretty

SCENE 6   FOLLOW THAT GIRL   27

1st Girl Bystander (*who carries a parasol*)
    Goodness, how tragic
2nd Girl Bystander.
    She has a magic
3rd Girl Bystander.
    Is she intending
    An unhappy ending?
All the Bystanders.
    Don't!
    Solitary Stranger,
    Where did you come from?
    What have you run from?
    Did you do something wrong?
    Can you be in danger?
    Let us befriend you
    Couldn't we send you
    Back to where you belong?

(Tom *enters down* L. *He and* Victoria *gaze at each other. Slowly* Victoria *comes down and moves towards him,* LC. Tom *puts out his hands to welcome her*)

Tom.   Solitary Stranger,
    Are you in hiding?
    Are you deciding
    Here you will spend your days
    And be a solitary stranger
    Always.

(*The music changes to the chase.* Victoria *looks about her terrified, as* Tancred *and* Wilberforce *enter* R. *As they move towards Victoria,* Mr Gilchrist *enters* L, *closely followed by* Mrs Gilchrist. *They all grab at Victoria. Terrified,* Victoria *runs to the parapet, seizes the parasol from the 1st Girl Bystander, climbs to the top and jumps. She "floats" in the air for a moment, buoyed up by the open parasol, before she gently glides out of view, down the ramp.* Tom *is momentarily transfixed in horror. The* Bystanders *run to the parapet and look over*)

Bystanders (*in terror*) Ooooh! (*They watch the fall; does she hit the water? In "Oh-what-a-shame" tone*) Aaaaaaah! (*The direction of their stares suggests a gust of wind may have caught the open parasol. In surprise*) Ooooooh! (*They watch for a moment, as if she is drifting down river, then turn away*)

Cora.   Solitary Stranger,
    Did we deceive you?
    How can we leave you
    Lying beneath the foam?
    Come back, dear solitary stranger!
All.   Come home!

(*On the last note* Tom *is galvanized into action, takes a running bound up the steps and follows Victoria over the edge. The* Bystanders *discuss*

c

the tragedy with a quiet detachment. Mrs Gilchrist *weeps and is comforted by* Mr Gilchrist. Tancred *and* Wilberforce *are indignant at having spent so much energy in their chase to no purpose*)

Wilberforce. It's too bad of her, it really is.
Tancred. Just when I thought we'd got her!
Wilberforce. It's not fair. Girls can't go flying off on umbrellas whenever they feel like it. It's cowardice.
Tancred. Escapism.
Wilberforce. Are we going to give her up?
Tancred. Oh, no! We're British, aren't we?
Wilberforce. Of course. I almost forgot.

(Mr Gilchrist *exits* L)

"VICTORIA, VICTORIA"   No. 8

Tancred *and* Wilberforce (*singing, together*)
　　　　　　　Oh, have you seen Victoria?
Chorus.　　　Victoria, Victoria,
Tancred *and* Wilberforce.
　　　　　　　The girl we want to marry
　　　　　　　Has decided to depart.
Chorus.　　　Oh what is your Victoria,
　　　　　　　Victoria, Victoria?
Tancred *and* Wilberforce.
　　　　　　　She's full of grace and fair of face
　　　　　　　Our own sweetheart.
Cora (*stepping forward*)
　　　　　　　Oh, where is that policeman?
Chorus.　　　That policeman, that policeman,
Cora.　　　　He reminded me of somebody
　　　　　　　I can't remember who.
All.　　　　　We're looking for Victoria,
　　　　　　　Victoria, Victoria,
Tancred *and* Wilberforce.
　　　　　　　The girl we want to marry
Cora.　　　　And the boy in blue.
Mrs Gilchrist (*stepping forward*)
　　　　　　　Oh, have you seen Victoria?
All.　　　　　Victoria, Victoria,
Mrs Gilchrist. She left her home misguidedly
　　　　　　　And now she's "blown" away.
All.　　　　　Oh, what is your Victoria,
　　　　　　　Victoria, Victoria?
Mrs Gilchrist. A daughter who is going to turn me
　　　　　　　Prematurely grey.
Cora (*indicating Tancred and Wilberforce*)
　　　　　　　Oh, these are malefactors
　　　　　　　And we ought to run them in!
Mrs Gilchrist. Yes, a pair of malefactors
　　　　　　　They've committed every sin!

TANCRED and WILBERFORCE.	
	But we're looking for Victoria
	Victoria, Victoria,
	So wouldn't it be best
	To forget we're malefactors
	And to join the quest.
ALL.	Oh, have you seen Victoria,
	Victoria, Victoria,
	She might be almost anywhere
	So where do we begin?
	We're seeking a policeman,
	A policeman, a policeman,
	He was following Victoria
	And jumped right in.

(*The* BYSTANDERS *and* PRINCIPALS *move forward, and the* RUNNING TABS *close behind them*)

MRS GILCHRIST.	Oh, a mother's lost a daughter
CORA.	And another's lost a son.
ALL.	And today's a day when everyone
	Is losing everyone
	And we haven't seen Victoria,
	Victoria, Victoria,
	A lovely erring daughter
	And a long-lost son.
	Ah . . .

(*The* BYSTANDERS *remain as the* PRINCIPALS *exit. The music ends with a Round*)

"LOST, STOLEN OR STRAYED" No. 9

BYSTANDERS.	Lost, stolen or strayed
	A man and a fair young maid.
	A daughter and son have undutifully gone
	Lost, stolen or strayed.
	Bom!

Beginning at the start of the last line of the Round, the LIGHTS *slowly dim to* BLACK-OUT *on the last "Bom!" The* BYSTANDERS *exit and the* RUNNING TABS *open.*

SCENE 7

The scene is the Aquarium at London Zoo. A cut-cloth, hung at about half-stage depth, shows a number of fish-display tanks, greeny-blue and mysterious. The perspective suggests that this is a long, rather gloomy room, and the tanks stretch far back. In the centre a large oblong cut represents the front of a tank which is given central prominence, for it is the Keeper's pride and joy. It is is labelled PISCIS FEMINA BELISSIMA. *The cut is covered with a gauze which can be raised independently of the Aquarium front-cloth, and behind the gauze is a rock-piece, large enough to provide cover and sitting accommodation for three mermaids. This is masked either with a screen, enclosing the area of the tank, or with a cloth depicting the far side of the tank. The area thus enclosed must be lit, from above, independently of the rest of the set. A bench stands* LC.

When the LIGHTS *come slowly up, the stage is empty and the central tank remains in darkness. The whole effect is dim and aqueous, with glimpses of strange fish that reflect gleams of blue and green light; it could almost be underneath a strangely clean and exotic Thames.* VICTORIA *enters down* R *with a slow, floating, swimming motion. She looks round curiously, believing she must be under water. She "swims" up towards the tank* C. *The* KEEPER *enters down* R, *sweeping with a broom. He bears a quite remarkable resemblance to Mr Gilchrist, but lacks his dictatorial manner. He moves* RC, *sweeping, and then notices Victoria.*

KEEPER. What are you doing out there?

(VICTORIA *starts, rather guiltily, turns, and "settles", as if completing a long swim*)

Get back in your tank!

(VICTORIA *stares at him*)

Oh, sorry, miss. I thought at first you was a mermaid. Of course I can see you haven't got a tail. That'll be sixpence please.

VICTORIA (*crossing to the Keeper's* L) What for?

KEEPER. It's the regulation, miss.

VICTORIA. I'm sorry, but I haven't any money on me. I didn't think I'd need it. I thought I'd be dead, you see.

KEEPER. Why?

VICTORIA. Well, I jumped, you see, from Albert Bridge, and I should really be drowned by now. I wonder what saved me.

(TOM, *dressed as the author, enters down* L)

TOM. It was your umbrella.

(*The moment Tom speaks, the* KEEPER *freezes and remains quite motionless until Tom has gone.* VICTORIA *turns to Tom and moves to down* R *of him*)

VICTORIA. What?

TOM. That red umbrella. Don't you remember? You snatched it from a bystander just before you jumped.

VICTORIA. But you jumped too, and you weren't carrying a red umbrella. Why aren't you drowned?

TOM. I changed my mind, just before I hit the water.

VICTORIA. Coward!

TOM. Not at all. It was entirely for artistic reasons. Have you ever seen the bottom of the Thames?

VICTORIA. Not that I'm aware of.

TOM. You'd hate it, honestly you would. So I arranged for the wind to carry you here.

SCENE 7   FOLLOW THAT GIRL   31

VICTORIA. Thank you. Where am I?
TOM. The Aquarium at London Zoo.
VICTORIA. That's the Keeper, I suppose?
TOM. Yes. He'll show you round if you ask him nicely. (*He kisses her and turns to go. He hesitates, turns to face Victoria again and speaks defensively*) It's perfectly possible, you know.
VICTORIA. What is?
TOM. To be carried through the air by an umbrella.
VICTORIA (*laughing*) I'm sure it is.

(TOM *exits down* L. VICTORIA *crosses to the Keeper's* L. *The* KEEPER *comes back to life*)

It's a beautiful aquarium.
KEEPER. Like it?
VICTORIA (*moving down* R *as she looks around*) You must have every fish there is.
KEEPER (*breaking* L) Just about. We've got angels and devils, and cuttles and swords . . .
VICTORIA. Got any mermaids?
KEEPER. Ah! That's a sore point. (*Pointing up* C) See this tank?
VICTORIA (*crossing up to the tank* C) Yes, but it's quite empty.
KEEPER. My dream tank. It's waiting for them.
VICTORIA. The mermaids?
KEEPER. There are plenty about, you know. But at the moment there's only one in captivity.
VICTORIA (*crossing to* R *of the Keeper*) Where is she?
KEEPER (*sadly*) Moscow. Of course, the Americans pretended they had one too, but any fool could see it was the top half of a monkey stitched on to the bottom half of a dolphin. You wouldn't catch me cheating the public like that.

(VICTORIA *takes the broom from the Keeper and leans it against the bench,* LC)

Thanks, dear.

(*They wander up stage together to* R *of the empty tank. They gaze at it reflectively*)

Oh, no, miss! There won't be anything doubtful about my mermaids.
VICTORIA. I feel very sorry for them: having people stare at them all the time.
KEEPER. They'll love it.

(*In relaxed and friendly conversation they cross and exit* L. *As soon as their backs are turned, the black backing behind the tank gauze flies away, and the* LIGHTS *go up behind the gauze revealing that the tank is now occupied by* MERCIA, MAVIS *and* MAUD, *three Victorian mermaids, who are sitting on the rock.* MERCIA *holds a mirror and is applying mascara to her luscious eyelashes;* MAVIS *has a mirror too, and is combing her golden tresses;* MAUD *is dabbing on a little rouge*)

"THREE VICTORIAN MERMAIDS"   No. 10

ALL (*singing*) Three Victorian Mermaids
MERCIA. Mercia!
MAVIS. Mavis!
MAUD. And Maud.
ALL. Three zoological showgirls
We're frustrated
Deflated
MAUD. And bored.
ALL. Our days in this aquarium
Are mainly spent in dreaming
Of how we'd like to vary 'em
By breaking the glass and screaming.

(*The* GAUZE *front of the tank* FLIES AWAY)

We long to be back in action
For we are the kind of girls
Who just adore
Eating oysters by the score
And throwing away the pearls.
We may be the main attraction
But goodness how we curse yer
When the population gawks
With its eyes on stalks
At
Mavis
Maud
And Mercia.

Three Victorian Mermaids
MERCIA. Mercia,
MAVIS. Mavis,
MAUD. And Maud.
ALL. Proud of our vital statistics.
MERCIA. Thirty-eight
MAVIS. Twenty-two
MAUD. Oh Lord!
ALL. When we three sang to the ships above
They would sink of their own sweet freewill
And then we'd say in tones of love
"The sea shall not have them, but we will."

We're Queens of the high and wide kicks
Or that's what the Navy said
Every British tar
Loves to cha-cha-cha
On a great big ocean bed.
We once were the sailor's side-kicks
And we can't think how the Navy's

                    Going to do without the zip
                    Of a
                    (*They twitch their tails, in turn*)
                        flop, flap, flip,
                    With Mercia, Maud, and Mavis.

(*Leaving their tails behind them, they abandon the concealment provided by the rock-piece, and prove to be wearing fish-net tights. They parade through the cut-cloth and "escape" on to the main body of the stage, where they dance*)

ALL. Well, we ask you.
         Don't you think it's a bit too much, girls?
         We're charming as you'll agree.
MAUD. When I used my wiles
         Mister Bernard Miles
         Named a theatre after me.
ALL.   But here we're the "Please-Don't-Touch"-Girls
         And it's no use getting bawdy
         'Cause how *can* you make a pass
         Through a wall of glass
         At

(*They return to the tank and resume their original poses*)

MERCIA. Mercia,
MAVIS.   Mavis,
MAUD.   And Maudie.

(*As the number ends, the* LIGHTS *on the tank snap* OUT, *and the* GAUZE *is dropped in again, followed by the* BLACK BACKING. VICTORIA *and the* KEEPER *enter down* L, *still deep in conversation*)

VICTORIA. They were all after me—my father, and Mr Tancred, and Mr Wilberforce, and a painter, and a policeman, and I'd promised to marry them; but of course I couldn't do that, so I just grabbed somebody's umbrella and jumped, and the wind carried me all the way here. (*She picks up the broom*)
KEEPER. Sit down, my dear. (*Taking the broom*) Thanks. We'll have some tea in a moment. It'll soon be feeding time.
VICTORIA (*sitting on the bench*) I feel so safe here. Perhaps I could stay and become one of your mermaids.
KEEPER (*moving* C) Nothing I'd like better. But it's not as easy as all that. It isn't just a question of growing a tail, you know.
VICTORIA (*rising and crossing to* R *of the Keeper*) Really? I always thought it was.
KEEPER. Oh, no, my dear. There's much more to it than that.

"MERMAID SCALES"   No. 11

KEEPER (*singing*)
         If you really want to be a mermaid
         If you want to make the sea your home

>   You are not allowed to wear
>   Any clothes except your hair
>   Which will take you more than half a day to comb
>   Here's a hint I always give prospective mermaids
>   It's a maxim of my aunt's which never fails
>   If a mermaid wants a merman
>   Then the way to make him her man
>   Is to polish up her mermaid scales
>   (*He cups his* R *ear as* VICTORIA *rehearses*)

VICTORIA. Doh Re Mi
KEEPER. I can't hear you at all.
VICTORIA. *Doh Re Mi*
KEEPER. Did I tell you to bawl?
VICTORIA. Doh Re Mi
BOTH (*together*) I'm (You're) singing a mermaid scale
VICTORIA. Doh Re Mi
KEEPER. Make it clear as a bell.
VICTORIA. Doh Re Mi
KEEPER. Good, you're doing it well.
VICTORIA. Doh Re Mi
BOTH (*together*) I'm (You're) singing a mermaid scale
KEEPER. You will have to learn to fence with a swordfish

(VICTORIA *tries a few practice thrusts and parries, up* L)

>   And bubble and squeak with the whales.
>   But you never can become an adored fish
>   Till you polish up your mermaid scales
>   Fa Mi Re

VICTORIA (*facing front*)
          Doh Re Mi
KEEPER. Sing it right from the heart
VICTORIA. Doh Re Mi
KEEPER. Pretty good for a start
VICTORIA. Doh Re Mi
BOTH (*together*) I'm (You're) singing a mermaid scale

(*The* KEEPER *crosses down to* R *of Victoria*)

KEEPER. If you really want to be a mermaid
        You will have to keep a dogfish as a pet
        And I usually tell a
        (*Raising the broom, which* VICTORIA *gratefully "shelters" under*)
        Girl to bring an umbrella
        Cause the sea's inclined to be a trifle wet.
        (*He lowers the broom and pauses for a moment*)
        As I've said the chief attraction of a mermaid
        Is a voice that causes porpoises to leap
        And every day you oughta
        Gargle with salt water
        If you want to be the Callas of the Deep

VICTORIA (*facing down* L)
    Doh Re Mi
KEEPER. Tones a little bit crude
VICTORIA. *Doh Re Mi*
KEEPER. There's no need to be rude.
VICTORIA. Doh Re Mi
BOTH (*together*) I'm (You're) singing a mermaid scale
VICTORIA (*facing front*)
    Doh Re Mi
KEEPER. Keep it charming and light
VICTORIA. Doh Re Mi
KEEPER. Now you're getting it right.
VICTORIA. Doh Re Mi
BOTH (*together*) I'm (You're) singing a mermaid scale

(VICTORIA *crosses to* R *of the* Keeper, *and both move down stage. As they complete the Musical Number, the* RUNNING TABS *close behind them*)

KEEPER. When you marry I will give you a trousseau
    Of everyday and evening tails
    Just as long as when I tell you to do so
    You polish up your mermaid scales
    Fa Mi Re
VICTORIA. Doh Re Mi.
KEEPER. Now you're simply sublime.
VICTORIA. Doh Re Mi.
KEEPER. Years ahead of her time
VICTORIA. Doh Re Mi.
BOTH. We're singing a mermaid scale.
    Doh Re Mi Fa So La Te Doh
    Let's keep singing it
    Let's keep swinging it
    Let's keep singing a mermaid scale!

The LIGHTS BLACK-OUT. VICTORIA *and the* KEEPER *exit. The Music for Scene 8 begins.*

SCENE 8

"SONG AND DANCE"   No. 12

A SPOT *picks up* TOM *who is standing* C *stage. He is in police uniform again, and is on point duty, directing traffic. The* RUNNING TABS *open after a moment, and* TOM *walks up into a full-stage set.*
The scene is City Centre. It is late at night so black velvet drapes or a special night back-drop takes the place of the skycloth. A cut-out, up C, *suggests we might be in Piccadilly Circus, looking towards Eros. Enterprising stage electricians may care to fix a few practical street-lamps of an antiquated pattern. If there is room, there can be a small stand belonging to a newspaper-seller, even a barrow-boy parked well out of the way, and*

any other oddments to suggest this is the busy heart of the city on a warm Edwardian summer's night. But there must be plenty of stage space remaining for movement and dancing.

When the RUNNING TABS *open the stage is full of* PASSERS-BY, *busily pursuing their own ways, and* TOM *has some difficulty in controlling the traffic as they cross and recross, generally interrupting his work.*

TANCRED *and* WILBERFORCE *enter up* R. *They are in disguise and carry sandwich-boards bearing the legend* WILBERTAN BABY SOAP. *They move down* R *and cross to* RC, *and a little knot of people gathers round as they cry their wares.*

TANCRED. Buy Wilbertan Baby Soap! On sale at Tancred's! Only fourpence!
WILBERFORCE. Wilbertan Baby Soap! Get it at Wilberforce's! Only threepence-halfpenny!
TANCRED. Baby Soap! Threepence!
WILBERFORCE. One penny!

(TOM *gets angry and moves down, scattering the crowd*)

TOM. Move along there!

(*The* PASSERS-BY *disperse, grumbling a little, and* TANCRED *and* WILBERFORCE *continue on their way to exit down* L. *For a moment,* TOM *is alone*)

"SONG AND DANCE"

TOM (*singing*)
  A constable
  Has traffic to direct
  A constable
  Has people to protect
  And every passer-by
  Thinks
  A constable
  Is someone you expect
  To know what's what
  To know the lot
  Or he'll know the reason why

(*The stage begins to fill again as* PASSERS-BY *enter, cross and exit, then re-enter. Some stop to ask Tom questions, to his exasperation*)

  Don't make a song and dance about it
  Keep the road clear!
1ST LADY PASSER-BY (*spoken*)
  Assist me!
TOM. Why can't you leave a crazy young fella be?
1ST GENTLEMAN PASSER-BY (*spoken*)
  This map isn't sense!
TOM. If you've a trouble, must you shout it
  Right in my ear?

SCENE 8   FOLLOW THAT GIRL

2ND LADY PASSER-BY (*dragging a* YOUNG GENTLEMAN *with her; spoken*)
    He kissed me!
TOM.   Nothing's achieved by raising up hell at me.
2ND GENTLEMAN PASSER-BY (*spoken*)
    Where's the nearest Gents?
TOM.   I'm not *your* policeman
    Are we poor policemen
    Just your Universal
    Aunts—
1ST GENTLEMAN PASSER-BY (*spoken*)
    —Yes!—
TOM.   —I doubt it
    If you must make a song and dance about it
    Don't make it here!
    (*He crosses down* L)
    Don't make
    A song and dance!
    Song and dance!

(WALTER *and* CORA *enter down* L *and cross to* C)

WALTER.   Constable, Constable,

(TOM *returns to meet them* C)

    Find my painting!
    My wife is nearly fainting
    Constable, Constable,

(MRS GILCHRIST *enters down* R *and crosses to* TOM'S L)

    Find my work of art!
MRS GILCHRIST.
    Constable, Constable,
    Find my daughter!
    She jumped into the water
    Constable, Constable,
    Mend a broken heart!
1ST GENTLEMAN PASSER-BY (*sung*)
    Tell me the time!
2ND GENTLEMAN PASSER-BY.
    I've lost my way!
3RD LADY PASSER-BY.
    My little dog
    Has gone astray!
4TH LADY PASSER-BY.
    See me across
    This dangerous road!
TOM.   Why don't you learn the Highway Code?

(TANCRED *and* WILBERFORCE *hurry on down* L. *They have shed their sandwich-boards but are still disguised*)

TANCRED *and* WILBERFORCE (*together*)
>Constable, Constable,
>People chase us!
>They're trying to disgrace us!
>What do we do?
>We depend on you.

ALL (*except Tom*)
>What do we do?

(TOM *is now harried by the entire* COMPANY. *He repeats the refrain, while the crowd pesters him*)

TOM.	ALL THE OTHERS.
Don't make a song and dance about it	Constable, Constable, Find that painting!
Keep the road clear!	This lady's nearly fainting
Why can't you leave a crazy young fella be?	Constable, Constable, Find that work of art!
If you're in trouble, must you shout it	Constable, Constable, Find that daughter!
Right in my ear?	She jumped into the water
Nothing's achieved by raising up hell at me	Constable, Constable, Mend a broken heart!
I'm not	Tell me the time!
your policeman	I've lost my way!
Are we	My little dog
poor policemen	Has gone astray!
Just your	See me across
Universal Aunts?	This dangerous road I never read the
I doubt it.	Highway Code.
If you must make a song and dance about it	Constable, Constable, Can you hear us?
Don't make it here!	We want to keep you near us
Don't make	What do we do?
A song and dance!	We depend on you
Song and dance!	What do we do?

(TOM *breaks through them and takes his helmet off*)

TOM.   As author I've a right to interfere
I'm sick of you!
(*He faces up stage*)
Skedaddle! Disappear!
(*He moves up* C)

(*Almost at once* TOM *is left alone on stage as the others glide away,* L *and* R. VICTORIA *enters up* L *and crosses to* Tom, *up* C)

VICTORIA. You can't do that.
TOM. Can't I?

SCENE 8 — FOLLOW THAT GIRL

VICTORIA. Of course not. It's a confession of failure. Call them back and sort them out! They'll do as you say!
TOM. So they will.

(VICTORIA *runs up stage to beckon the* COMPANY *to return to the stage.* TOM *points to the drums in the orchestra pit and the rhythm of the number begins again. The* COMPANY *enter and advance on* TOM)

VICTORIA.   COMPANY.
          (*singing, together*)

Constable, Constable,	Let's make a song and
Author, Author,	Dance about it
We hope that	Let's make a row—
You'll bring forth a	
Beautiful, suitable	Something's about that's
Ending to our	Getting to scare the
Woes.	Town—scare the town—
Constable, Constable,	As for convention
Master, Master,	We shall flout it
It seems that	You've shown us how—
You have cast a	
Spell upon all of our	And with a shout we're
Voices and our	Letting our hair right
Toes	Down—right down!

TOM (*singing*)
Give me a rest, I	We are
Need to think	What you make us
Don't be a pest, I'll	You've just
Take to drink	Got to take us
I thought you up, from	By the
Out of my brain	Hand, we've not a
I'd like to think you	Chance, with—
Down again	—out it

TOM, VICTORIA *and*   GIRLS.
    MALE CHORUS.
          (*singing together*)

So we	Constable, Constable,
Must make a song and	Can you hear us?
Dance about it	We want to
Let's make it now—	Keep you near us
	What do we do?—
Let's make——	

ALL (*together*)
         A Song and Dance
         Song and Dance
         Song and Dance.

         The CURTAIN *falls*

ACT II

Scene 1

The scene is the Author's Flat, as at the opening of Act I.

When the Curtain *rises,* Victoria *in her modern dress is squatting on the floor below the armchair,* R. *She looks very cosy and comfortable and has taken off her shoes.* Tom *is sitting in the armchair with the script on his lap. The* Lights *are dim, so we do not notice that* Tom *is dressed as a policeman from the waist down. He and* Victoria *are drinking beer out of plastic mugs.*

Tom. More beer?

Victoria. No, thanks. I really ought to be getting home, Tom. Father will be livid.

Tom. But we're only half-way through.

Victoria. All right. Tell me quickly what happens in the second half. How does it begin?

Tom (*rising*) Don't know. (*He moves* C *and paces back and forth*) Haven't decided yet. (*He tucks the script under one arm*) Shall I bring on the chorus again? (*He shapes as if to clap his hands*) It's easily done.

Victoria (*signalling to him*) No, let them have a rest, poor things. I'm sure they must be tired after that song and dance bit. Besides, I think you ought to get back to the plot.

Tom (*fumbling through the script and letting a page fall to the floor*) Ah yes, the plot. Where on earth *is* the plot? I had a synopsis somewhere.

Victoria (*picking up the loose page and sitting in the armchair*) Is this it? (*She reads from the page*) One frantic hero——

Tom (*moving behind the armchair and looking over her shoulder*) One distraught heroine——

Victoria. Two foolish suitors chasing said heroine——

Tom. One elderly couple looking for lost picture——

Victoria. Secondly elderly couple——

(Mrs Gilchrist *enters down* L)

——looking for lost daughter——
(*She freezes as* Mrs Gilchrist *speaks*)

Mrs Gilchrist. A little less of the *elderly*, if you don't mind.

Tom (*putting the script gently on to Victoria's lap*) Oh, so you've decided to open the second act for us.

Mrs Gilchrist. Certainly. Unless, of course, you've something *better* to suggest.

Tom. No, no. Nothing at all. Do carry on.

Mrs Gilchrist. Thank you. (*As if to someone at the back of the auditorium*) Lights, please.

SCENE I FOLLOW THAT GIRL 41

(A SPOTLIGHT *comes up on* MRS GILCHRIST. *The* LIGHTING *on Victoria and the armchair dim quickly to* BLACK-OUT. *As Mrs Gilchrist speaks,* VICTORIA *exits* R, *and the armchair is removed.* TOM *steps into the wings and returns as soon as possible wearing his policeman's helmet and buttoning up his uniform jacket. The Streets of London* RUNNING TABS *close in. The* AUTHOR'S FLAT GAUZE *and* BACKING FLIES AWAY)

Meanwhile, Mrs Gilchrist, believing that she had lost her only daughter—(*she droops, applying a black-edged hanky to her eyes*) decided to seek consolation in a shopping expedition. (*She trots briskly to* C *stage, turns, and moves* L *again*) Her face wore an expression of smiling tragedy—(*she tries tragedy, then smiling, then tragedy again. She switches two or three times, but can't manage them both together*) too difficult. Her face was completely expressionless—(*this she manages*) but because she was blinded with tears, she could not read the names on the front of the shops. (*She gropes her way across stage towards* R *until she bumps into* TOM *who has now completed his quick change*) Excuse me, Constable, is this Tancred's Stores?
TOM. No, ma'am.

(*As he gives directions* MRS GILCHRIST *tries to follow them in mime but ends up hopelessly confused and giddy*)

Take the first turning on the right——
MRS GILCHRIST. Yes.
TOM. —then the second on the left——
MRS GILCHRIST. Yes.
TOM. —then—(*briskly*) best foot forward down Regent Street.
MRS GILCHRIST (*having great difficulty in deciding between her feet*) Yes.
TOM. Three times round Oxford Circus.
MRS GILCHRIST (*spinning*) Yes. Why three times?
TOM. For luck! Branch off sharply to the left...
MRS GILCHRIST. Ow!
TOM. Double back on your tracks...
MRS GILCHRIST (*running backwards*) Ye-e-es.
TOM. Follow your nose, close your eyes, think of the number you first thought of, and you're there!
MRS GILCHRIST (*faintly*) Thank you, Constable. You've been most helpful—(*she staggers towards* R *stage, deciding to take a cab after all, and hailing one in a defeated voice*) Cabby! (*She exits* R)
TOM (*gleefully rubbing his hands*) That'll teach her not to push authors around! (*He exits* L)

(*The* LIGHTS *begin to build up to daylight.* TANCRED *and* WILBERFORCE *enter* R, *mopping their brows*)

WILBERFORCE. I say, Tancred...
TANCRED. Yes, Wilber?
WILBERFORCE. Rather warm, what?
TANCRED. Whta? Oh, yes, positively perspiratious. Must be the sun that's doing it.
WILBERFORCE. Too warm for chasing, what?

TANCRED. Better for strolling, what, what?
WILBERFORCE. What, what, what?
TANCRED (*yelling*) Better for strolling?

"LET'S TAKE A STROLL" No. 13

TANCRED *and* WILBERFORCE (*singing, together*)
    Let's take the afternoon off
    It's time we had some fun
TANCRED.   Temp'rature's in the eighties
WILBERFORCE It's much too hot to run.
BOTH.   It's not the kind of a day
    For going fast or far

(*Two* GIRLS *enter, with parasols. They wear summery dresses and look very pretty*)

    But there's one thing we *can* do
    Right now and just as we are

(*During the refrain* TANCRED *and* WILBERFORCE *flirt with the* GIRLS *who, after a proper show of disinterest, join them*)

    Let's take a stroll through London
    And look about us idly as we go
    We'll sit under trees
    Or wander at our ease
    In surprising bits of London
    That we didn't know!
    Let's take a stroll through London
    To saunter is a lordly thing to do
TANCRED, WILBERFORCE *and* GIRLS (*together*)
    Oh, this is the way
    To spend a holiday
    When the grass is green in London
    And the sky is blue!

(*Two more* COUPLES *enter and join the Girls and the two truant suitors*)

ALL (*singing*)
    Hand in hand
    We'll wander down the Mall
    Or chatter with the pigeons in the Square
    In summertime
    For every boy and gal
    There's nothing like a breath of London air
    Come on then!

    Let's take a stroll through London
    Explore it from the Palace to the Zoo.
    Oh, this is the way

> To spend a holiday
> When the grass is green in London
> And the sky is blue!

(*They parade off,* L, *as a group of* COCKNEY BOYS *and* GIRLS *enter* R *to take up the refrain*)

COCKNEYS (*singing*)
> Let's take a stroll through London
> Our feet are bound to lead us Lambeth way
> Then up to the 'Eath
> To see the town beneath
> With the roof-tops all a-glitterin'
> So bright and gay
> Let's take a stroll through London
> And when we're tired I'll tell you what we'll do
> We'll jump on a bus
> That's empty but for us
> And we'll see the bloomin' lilacs
> Bloomin' down at Kew
>
> We'll smile at old
> Big Ben and 'ear 'im chime
> And take in Nelson's Column comin' back;
> Round Leicester Square
> And then, if we've the time,
> We'll visit Auntie Lil—
> (She lives at 'Ackney Marshes)
>
> Let's take a stroll through London
> From the Elephant and Castle to the Strand
> There's no nicer way
> To spend a holiday
> Than to take a stroll through dear old London
> Hand in hand!

They all stroll happily away, R *and* L, *as the* RUNNING TABS *open to reveal:*

SCENE 2

The scene is the interior of Tancred's Store, the Ladies' Wear Department, probably on the second floor. Although this is a rather more elaborate set than others in the play it needn't be over-realistic or too heavy. The permanent wings or legs remain, with a notice or two indicating that other departments of the store are off R *and* L. *The backcloth shows that the interior wall of the department is richly decorated, for this is a high-class emporium. At* RC *a notice on the wall reads "The Management accepts no responsibility for anything that happens in this Establishment".*

The set is dressed with a variety of display stands, counters, dummy models and stylish Victorian wares and fashions, more or less as desired, but the following features are essential: a number of wire baskets, stacked down R (*Tancred's is now self-service*), *and above them an upright chair with padded seat. Mid-stage* R, *a small counter with a number of hats on a display, and above this a counter piled with packets of stockings. On this counter two model "legs" show stockings and garters to advantage. Up* R *is a light, easily movable screen, just deep enough to observe the proprieties for those who try on gowns behind it. Across the back a number of dummy models are tastefully grouped, displaying gowns of the day. One of the gowns is black, and has a train. Up* C *stage is a double-sided mirror on a stand, set edge-on to the audience. Prominently on view up* L *is a model displaying a rather dashing black corset and below this is a counter offering a quantity of pairs of shoes. Mid-stage* L *stands a figure showing a fur coat. Down* L *is a desk on which there is an ornate comptometer, and behind the desk is a stool.*

When the RUNNING TABS *open,* MISS PAYTON, *the cashier, is seated behind the desk down* L. *The department is full of* LADY SHOPPERS, *accompanied by one or two disgruntled* HUSBANDS, BROTHERS *or* SONS, *who are all parading round the store.*
 The music continues and they sing.

SHOPPERS.   Let's take a stroll through Tancred's
            And wander while we ponder what to buy
            We do so adore
            Parading round a store
            Where we know the goods are good
            Because the price is high
            Let's stop at every counter
            And help ourselves to something on the way
            Then what do we do?
MISS PAYTON. You *get* into the queue!
SHOPPERS.   Oh, of course, we'd quite forgotten
            That we *have* to pay!

(*Some of the* SHOPPERS *queue up to pay* MISS PAYTON, *who is soon busily employed at the comptometer. The machine issues receipts from a strip, the length varying slightly according to the value of each purchase*)

            Here we see
            Arrayed on every shelf
            The best that Mr Tancred can provide
            We agree
            It's fun to serve one's self

(*A* YOUNG WIFE *steps forward, dragging her* HUSBAND *by the arm*)

YOUNG WIFE. It's all so nice I'm taking twice
            The time deciding!

(*Her* HUSBAND *has had enough and pushes her into the paying-up queue*)

ALL.	Let's take a stroll through Tancred's
It's easier for wives to settle down
After they've been
To see and to be seen
On a shopping expedition in the
Heart of London Town!

(*Most of the* SHOPPERS *have paid, and leave the department,* R *and* L; *a few remain, selecting small purchases. Amongst them is a* WOMAN *who has been examining the fur coat on the model mid-stage* L. *She now removes it from the model and presents it at the cash-desk.* MISS PAYTON *bangs the comptometer which issues a bill so long that the* WOMAN *has to coil it round into her basket as it pours forth. When it stops, with a final spurt,* MISS PAYTON *tears off the bill and the* WOMAN *examines the total*)

WOMAN. Put it on my account, please. (*She picks up the fur coat and exits up* L)

(MISS PAYTON *notices that the model which wore the fur coat now looks rather bare in a skimpy dust-cover. She crosses* R *to the hat counter and chooses a little black pork-pie hat and is returning to the model* L *when* MRS GILCHRIST *enters down* R *and looks round her uncertainly*)

MRS GILCHRIST. Good morning. You are—open?
MISS PAYTON (*pausing at* LC) Yes, Madam. The baskets are over there. (*She indicates down* R, *then goes to the model* L, *poises the little black hat at a jaunty angle on the model, and returns to her cash-desk*)
MRS GILCHRIST. Oh, I don't want a basket. (*She stands close to the pile of baskets, facing towards Miss Payton, waiting to be served*)

(*A* CUSTOMER-IN-A-HURRY, *her basket on her arm, enters down* R. *She turns to collect a wire basket and her own basket bumps Mrs Gilchrist in the back. She turns once more and this time the wire basket catches Mrs Gilchrist rather harder in the same place.* MRS GILCHRIST *is propelled to* C *stage. She turns to remonstrate with her assailant, but the* CUSTOMER-IN-A-HURRY *has moved up to the stocking counter and is collecting several packets which she thrusts into the wire basket.* MRS GILCHRIST *is appalled, turns to Miss Payton and coughs discreetly. There is no reaction so she moves closer to the cash-desk*)

MRS GILCHRIST (*hissing confidentially*) Sssssst! I think I ought to tell you—that woman over there——

(*The* CUSTOMER-IN-A-HURRY *comes briskly across to the desk*)

(*The words sticking in her throat with embarrassment*) —she's shoplifting!

(MISS PAYTON *pays no attention, but accepts the* CUSTOMER'S *money and bangs the comptometer. The* CUSTOMER *transfers the stockings to her own basket and exits down* L. MRS GILCHRIST *stares after her in a bemused fashion, then returns* C, *taps her foot and coughs loudly*)

Oh dear, I *am* in rather a hurry. (*She moves towards Miss Payton a few steps*) Perhaps you could help me. You see, I need cheering up. I'm looking for something gay, pretty—not too frivolous, of course. . . .

Miss Payton (*hardly glancing up*) Help yourself, madam.
Mrs Gilchrist. I beg your pardon?
Miss Payton. We're Self-Service now, madam. (*Seeing she has not been understood, and enunciating with care*) One serves one's self.

(*For a moment* Mrs Gilchrist *looks mystified, then decides to interpret the advice literally. She returns* c *and issues the unctuous welcome of the old-style shop assistant*)

Mrs Gilchrist (*facing down* R) Good morning, modom; can I help you? (*Turning her head to face down* L) Thank you. I need something that will cheer me up. (*To down* R, *heartily*) Certainly, modom. What about a nice new titfer? (*To down* L) What a splendid idea! (*She removes her own hat, crosses briskly to the corset model, without examining it, and pops her hat incongruously on the model's head*) Would you step this way, modom? (*She crosses blithely up* R *and puts her umbrella over the arm of the right-hand model of the gown-display group, then moves down* R *to the chair where she deposits her handbag. She moves up to the hat counter and selects one*) Ah! The very thing for modom. (*Moving up to* R *of the mirror* c *and trying on the hat*) It suits you—yes, it really does suit you! (*Turning to look over her shoulder*) I suppose you haven't this style in black? (*Sadly looking in the mirror again*) I should be in mourning, you know—my daughter . . . (*She turns away*) No, on second thoughts, please don't bother. We'll try another. (*She returns the hat to the counter and gathers up an armful, goes to* L *of the mirror and tries on the hats in rapid succession*) No . . . no . . . no, not quite me. (*She collects them and returns them to the counter. Now she notices an enormous hat, with feathers*) Ooooh! I say! (*She can hardly lift it, and having set it on her head she almost crumples beneath the weight*) I made it! (*She staggers over to* Miss Payton) What do you think?

(Miss Payton *shakes her head pityingly*)

(*Turning away to* c) A little too noticeable, perhaps. What is everyone wearing this season? I must ask Victoria. Oh, what am I saying. (*She begins to weep, crosses* R *and returns the hat to the counter*) Oh, my little one! (*She turns sadly, notices the black pork-pie hat on the model* L, *and is instantly cheered*) Oooooo! (*She crosses to the hat*) I'll settle for this one. (*She plucks the hat from the model, crosses to look in the* L *side of the mirror and tries it on; approvingly*) Unobtrusive, but not without style. (*She moves down* R *to collect a wire basket*)

(*A* Determined Shopper *enters down* R. *As* Mrs Gilchrist *reaches for the top basket of the pile, the* Determined Shopper *gets there first and snatches the basket away*. Mrs Gilchrist, *silently indignant at this display of bad manners, watches balefully as the* Determined Shopper *crosses* LC. *Again,* Mrs Gilchrist *turns towards the baskets, and a* 2nd Determined Shopper *rushes in down* R. *This time* Mrs Gilchrist *just beats her to the draw, and gives her a triumphant, cocky smirk as she turns away up* R; *she is beginning to get the idea. The* 2nd Determined Shopper *crosses to examine the shoe counter, while* Mrs Gilchrist, *hoping nobody is watching, examines the gay garters on the*

SCENE 2   FOLLOW THAT GIRL   47

display "legs". Meanwhile, the 1ST DETERMINED SHOPPER *has chosen Mrs Gilchrist's hat from the corset model. She pays for it and walks out up* L *wearing it. At the last moment* MRS GILCHRIST *spots her and crosses as if to stop her; but this brings her face to face with the corset model, which she observes in detail for the first time*)

I say! (*Looking round cautiously*) Steady, Biddy. (*Very embarrassed she takes the corset off the stand*)

(*The* 2ND DETERMINED SHOPPER *has selected a pair of shoes and comes down to pay for them. She and* MISS PAYTON *observe Mrs Gilchrist's struggle with a dispassionate stare*)

(*Hiding the corset behind her*) Where does one—er—is there no privacy in this shop? (*She notices the screen, up* R) Oh, excuse me.

(*The* 2ND DETERMINED SHOPPER *pays for her purchase and exits down* L)

(*She crosses to the screen, drags it* C *stage, moves behind such cover as it provides and hangs a* "DO NOT DISTURB" *notice over the top*) Oh, husband! If you could see me now! (*She sinks out of sight*)

(EDWARD *and* EFFIE, *a young married couple enter from up* L *and cross to* C. EFFIE *is having the shopping spree of her life and is in the highest of spirits.* EDWARD *is already loaded down with two wire baskets filled with goods selected from other departments. He is exhausted and is not enjoying himself*)

EFFIE. What a lovely afternoon we're having! Don't you adore shopping, Edward. *I* do! (*She looks round predatorily and spots Mrs Gilchrist's umbrella on the model up* RC) Oh, Edward! Look! (*She crosses up* R) That umbrella! (*She unhooks it and brings it down* C *to Edward*) Isn't it absolutely the most delicious thing you've ever seen? (*She twirls it round, crossing to Edward's* L) I can't resist it. Well, I ask you, Edward, could you?

EDWARD. Just.

(EFFIE *hangs it over Edward's arm and flits around the shop gaily selecting this, that and the other and piling the goods into Edward's baskets. Every so often* MRS GILCHRIST *decides they are perilously close to her screen and shuffles with it into a new position. The young couple do not notice. The first of these moves takes* MRS GILCHRIST *up stage close to the gown display models, and she takes advantage of the opportunity to hang her own gown, which she has now managed to remove, over the arm of a model up* LC. *The second move takes her within reach of the model* L *which originally wore the fur coat.* MRS GILCHRIST'S *arm reaches out and puts a red slip on the model before being forced to move on, this time up to the stocking counter,* R. *Out of the corner of her eye,* EFFIE *catches sight of the screen and stares suspiciously for a moment. Then the old instinct takes over again and she moves to the screen enthusiastically*)

EFFIE. Isn't that a pretty screen, Edward? (*She moves it a little, and* MRS GILCHRIST *has to shuffle with it to remain concealed*) It exactly matches our dining-room curtains.

EDWARD (*dragging Effie towards the cash-desk*) Come on. We're going home.

(MRS GILCHRIST *takes advantage of the fact that* EFFIE *turns away to shuffle the screen back to the stocking counter*)

EFFIE. Oh, please, my darling, let me help myself to just one thing more and then your wicked Effie will be silent for ever.

EDWARD. Is that a promise?

(EFFIE *nods*)

Very well.

(EFFIE *looks greedily round the shop until her eyes light on Mrs Gilchrist's dress up* LC. *She crosses to it*)

EFFIE. This! (*She takes it off the model's arm*)

EDWARD. How much?

EFFIE (*crossing with* EDWARD *to the cash-desk*) It doesn't say, so we can pretend it's lovely and cheap, can't we?

(MISS PAYTON *prepares to check their heap of purchases*)

(*Suddenly having second thoughts and pointing down* L) Oh, Edward, look! The jewellery department! This dress just screams for a diamond necklace.

(EDWARD *wearily gathers the baskets again*)

(*Sweetly, to Miss Payton*) We'll pay through there. (*She leads off determinedly down* L. EDWARD *no longer has the strength to rebel, and follows her meekly*)

(*A* GIRL *enters down* R. *She looks at the screen by the stocking counter, moves to it, gathers it up and exits with it down* L. MRS GILCHRIST *is revealed, wearing the new black corset. In her hand she now holds her own pink corset. Suddenly, in a panic, she hears the voices of* CORA *and* WALTER MISKIN *approaching, down* R)

WALTER (*off*) Oh, do let's go in here. I love these self-help shops.

CORA. I love all shops, dear. But I think it's extravagant to buy the thing at all.

(MRS GILCHRIST *hastily rams her old corset over the "legs" on the stocking counter and hurries up* LC *to the model on which she had left her own dress. It's gone! Frantically she grabs for one of the other dresses on display. Too late!* WALTER *and* CORA *enter down* R. MRS GILCHRIST *turns and freezes into a pose similar to the models around her*)

WALTER. No, Cora, at your time of life such things become essential. (*He crosses* LC)

(CORA *moves up to examine the hat display*)

That Guinevere costume looks distressingly tight on you. (*He turns and notices Mrs Gilchrist's pink corset on the stocking counter. He crosses to above Cora*) Sh! The very thing!

(*For a moment their backs are turned as they take down the corset and examine it.* MRS GILCHRIST *struggles to get a black dress, with train, off the model beside her*)

CORA (*plaintively*) But, Walter, it seems such a waste of money when nobody will ever see it.

WALTER (*turning as he examines the garment*) Nonsense, Cora! You must make sure they do.

(MRS GILCHRIST *freezes again*)

CORA. Well, if you say so, dear . . .

WALTER (*noticing the black corset on the "model" up* LC) Perhaps you'd prefer the black. (*He crosses to* L *of Mrs Gilchrist, jogging her arm. He draws Cora's attention to the garment by giving it a light flip with the back of his hand. This catches* MRS GILCHRIST *amidships, and her face twists in an expression of helpless "you'll pay for that later" indignation*)

CORA (*moving up to the* R *of Mrs Gilchrist*) No, dear, there's something unpleasantly—(*she gives the corset a little tug*) French about it.

(MRS GILCHRIST *raises an eyebrow.* WALTER *moves away to* L)

(*Examining the "model's" face*) What very disagreeable expressions they give their dummies these days! (*She crosses in front of Mrs Gilchrist, following Walter to* L)

(MRS GILCHRIST *goes to swipe Cora, but* WALTER *turns up and she freezes again*)

WALTER. It's the fashion, dear.

CORA (*turning back to have a last look at the "model's" face*) Ugh! (*She crosses back to the stocking counter and picks up the pink corset*) Let's take this. We may be able to get a reduction on it. It looks distinctly shop-soiled.

(WALTER *crosses back to Mrs Gilchrist as* CORA *folds up the pink corset. He looks into Mrs Gilchrist's eyes, jogs her head slightly from side to side.* CORA *crosses to the cash-desk and presents the pink corset for payment.* WALTER *joins her at the desk.* MRS GILCHRIST *gratefully continues with her task of removing the black dress from the model, while* MISS PAYTON *deals with the Miskins.*

TANCRED *and* WILBERFORCE *enter down* R. *They wear black armbands and are carrying the picture stolen from the Miskins. They spot Cora and Walter at the cash-desk and look aghast. They stand the picture on the floor with it's back towards the Miskins, and both crouch down behind it.* WALTER *takes the receipt issued by the comptometer and* CORA *exits down* L *with the pink corset,* WALTER *following.*

TANCRED *and* WILBERFORCE *sigh with relief, stand, and move to the stocking counter, parking the picture against it.* MRS GILCHRIST *has struggled half-way into her new black dress when* TANCRED *and* WILBERFORCE *notice her, and become very obsequious*)

TANCRED (*crossing to* L *of Mrs Gilchrist*) Good afternoon, madam.

WILBERFORCE (*to her* R) Is madam serving herself?

TANCRED (*pulling her between them, facing towards Wilberforce*) Perhaps we can assist her.

(*They flutter fawningly round her, helping her into the dress and spreading the train to the best effect*)

WILBERFORCE. A perfect choice if I may say so.

TANCRED (*pulling Mrs Gilchrist round to face him*) It just *is*, madam, isn't it?

WILBERFORCE (*pulling her round again*) Oh, it absolutely is!

(MRS GILCHRIST *has stood enough and slaps at their hands in the way she used to slap Victoria's when she was a child. She pushes them away*)

TANCRED (*removing his hat and putting it on the corner of the mirror* C) So good of you to patronize my shop.

WILBERFORCE (*taking her arm, leading her conspiratorially to* R, *and speaking quietly*) Actually it's mine. He doesn't know it yet, but last night I took him over. Tancred's is now Wilberforce's. (*He turns to put his hat on the stocking counter*)

TANCRED (*coming to Mrs Gilchrist's* L *and leading her to* C, *secretly*) You may be interested to hear that I now own another premises. Last night Wilberforce's became Tancred's.

MRS GILCHRIST (*fuming dangerously*) I see.

(WILBERFORCE *returns to Mrs Gilchrist's* R)

Well, gentlemen, whoever this shop belongs to——

TANCRED
WILBERFORCE } (*together, proudly*) Me!

MRS GILCHRIST. ——it's a disgrace!

(*Their faces fall*)

Who is responsible?

TANCRED
WILBERFORCE } (*together, pointing*) He is.

MRS GILCHRIST. It is nothing but a den of thieves. First my dress was stolen and then, under my very eyes, my foundation was removed.

TANCRED (*wiping his brow*) Oh my hat!

MRS GILCHRIST (*glancing at the model* L) Yes, and my hat—now that you come to mention it. Well, sirs, what have you got to say to that?

TANCRED (*pointing up to the notice*) "The Management accepts no responsibility——

WILBERFORCE (*pointing to the notice*) "—for anything that happens in this establishment."

MRS GILCHRIST. I have half a mind to call the police——

(TOM *enters down* R)

—but I won't.

(TOM *exits down* R)

(*She crosses to the chair* R *and collects her handbag, then turns and makes for the exit up* L. *She pauses by the shoe counter, puts her handbag down on it, and turns to* TANCRED *and* WILBERFORCE *to issue a final threat*) However, gentlemen, I warn you, you will suffer for this.

(TANCRED *and* WILBERFORCE, *terrified, huddle together* RC)
Never again will you be invited to my musical evenings!

(TANCRED *and* WILBERFORCE *exchange glances of beaming delight*)

(*Advancing on them*) I have been insulted and humiliated. Self-Service indeed! (*She stands over them*)

(*A* LATE SHOPPER *hurries in up* R, *crosses to the shoe counter and with delighted surprise examines Mrs Gilchrist's handbag. Quickly she takes it to the cash desk*, MISS PAYTON *accepts payment, and the* LATE SHOPPER *exits at speed down* L)

I, who have never helped myself to anything except an occasional chocolate! If I have lost a daughter, you have lost a customer. (*She turns and sweeps back to the shoe counter*) I shall seek consolation from Mr Harrod.

TANCRED } (*together*) No!
WILBERFORCE

MISS PAYTON. Excuse me, madam; you haven't paid for that dress.

TANCRED (*turning to down* R) Help! Police!

(TOM *enters down* R)

WILBERFORCE (*to Tom*) This lady was attempting to leave without paying.

MRS GILCHRIST (*feeling for the place where she left her handbag, without looking round*) How dare you? I have every intention of paying.

(TOM *exits down* R)

My bag's gone! Where's my bag? (*She advances on* TANCRED *and* WILBERFORCE *again with such fury that they shoot their hands into the air as if this was a stick-up*) This is too much! (*She comes down* C) I've lost my daughter and my dress and my hat and my daughter and my umbrella and my corset and my dignity and my handbag in your store. And I thought you were gentlemen. Oh, Victoria, if only I could tell you how wrong I've been.

(VICTORIA *enters down* R, *trots slowly across the stage and exits down* L. TANCRED *and* WILBERFORCE *move down level with Mrs Gilchrist and all three gape after her. Deliberately* TANCRED *and* WILBERFORCE *remove their black arm-bands, pause only to collect their hats, and then trot after* VICTORIA. MRS GILCHRIST *starts towards the exit down* L, *beginning to undo her black dress as she does so. She turns up as* VICTORIA *trots on from up* L *and runs across the back of the stage to exit up* R)

Victoria! Wait for mother! (*She rushes after her*)

(MISS PAYTON, *still with the store's interests at heart, rises and follows hurriedly*)

MISS PAYTON. Madam, the bill! (*She follows Mrs Gilchrist off, up* R)

(TANCRED *and* WILBERFORCE *double back on down* L)

TANCRED. We've lost her.

WILBERFORCE. Well, we'll just jolly-well have to find her again, won't we?

REPRISE—"FOLLOW THAT GIRL"   No. 14

TANCRED *and* WILBERFORCE (*together, singing*)
>Follow that girl
>I'll have to
>Follow that girl
>That girl who
>Came into my life
>From nowhere
>Now I'll have to go where-
>Ever she goes
>I'll have to follow my nose
>Until the
>Day she is my wife
>I'll follow that girl

(TOM *enters down* R)

TOM.
>I never
>Knew a man could fall in love
>So suddenly
>But when she
>Ran away the only thought
>That came to me
>Was, I must

(*The gentlemen of the* CHORUS *enter and sing with Tom*)

>   —He must

GENTLEMEN.
>Follow that Girl,
> He's got to
>Follow that girl
>That girl is
>Definitely worth
>My ardour
>If she runs I'll run the harder.
>Right across the earth,
>I'll follow that girl.

(*The ladies of the* CHORUS *enter and whistle a few bars*)

ALL.
>Follow that girl,
>He'll have to
>Follow that girl
>That girl who
>Came into his life
>From nowhere

Now he'll have to go where-
Ever she goes.
He'll have to
Follow his nose
Until the
Day she is his wife
He'll follow that girl,
Follow That Girl.

As the Music ends, the chase is resumed and the LIGHTS dim to BLACK-OUT.
A front-cloth is dropped in.

REPRISE—"CHASE MUSIC"   No. 14A

SCENE 3

The scene is Outside Tancred's Store.

When the LIGHTS come up, WALTER and CORA are crossing slowly from RC towards C. VICTORIA enters R, runs across the stage and exits L. Realizing that Victoria is being followed, WALTER pulls CORA up stage, and they stand aside as the chase passes by. MRS GILCHRIST, managing the train of her new dress with some difficulty, enters R and exits L, followed by MISS PAYTON and then two GENTLEMEN of the CHORUS. WILBERFORCE and TANCRED are next to cross, and they are recognized.

WALTER. There they are!
CORA. The thieves who stole my baby!
WALTER. The portrait-snatchers! Help! Police!
CORA. Police!

(Two more GENTLEMEN of the CHORUS cross from R to L, and then TOM arrives)

Quick, follow us!
WALTER. This way, man!

(WALTER and CORA join the hunt and exit L, TOM following in a measured plod. Meanwhile VICTORIA has been right round the store and enters down R again. She crosses and exits L, followed by MISS PAYTON and two GENTLEMAN of the CHORUS. TOM now returns from down L, as TANCRED and WILBERFORCE enter R, followed by two more GENTLEMEN of the CHORUS. With an imperious wave of his hand TOM stops the flow of "traffic", and they all freeze in mid-step. TOM turns to the down L entrance and beckons. A YOUNG MOTHER enters L, pushing a pram. She wheels it carefully above the rock-still chasers, and parks it RC)

YOUNG MOTHER (to the baby) Mummy won't be a moment. She's just going in to do a teeny-weeny bit of shopping——

(Satisfied for her safety, TOM waves the hunt to continue and walks off down L. TANCRED and WILBERFORCE, followed by the two GENTLEMEN of the CHORUS, resume their cross and exit L)

—and baby's got to be very good——

(WALTER *and* CORA *enter* R, *and have run as far as* LC *when they check, look at each other, and turn back to the Young Mother*)

—while she's gone. (*She makes towards the exit* R)
WALTER (*in a voice of thunder*) Woman!

(*The* YOUNG MOTHER *stops in alarm and turns*)

You ought to be shot!
YOUNG MOTHER (*returning to* RC) I beg your pardon?
WALTER. Leaving babies lying about like that—littered all over the pavement. It's shameful! Anyone could snatch it. We could.
CORA. Oh, yes, easily. (*She peers longingly into the pram*)
WALTER. If you don't look out, we *will!*

(*The* YOUNG MOTHER *turns in terror, grabs the pram and wheels it off* R *as quickly as she can go.* CORA *stifles a sob*)

Cora, my love! Whatever's the matter?
CORA. That baby was so like . . .
WALTER. Hush, dearest. (*He comforts her*)

(TOM *enters down* L)

Well, Constable, caught any good crooks lately?
TOM. Afraid not, sir.
WALTER. We shall just have to leave the pursuit to you. My wife has had a severe emotional upset.
TOM. I'm sorry, sir.

(CORA *stares into Tom's face and goes to grip his arm*)

WALTER. Keep at it.
TOM. Yes, sir. (*He turns and exits* L)
CORA. Walter! Did you notice? He has a *very* powerful look of Cousin Herbert.
WALTER. That's funny. I saw another policeman this morning with a very powerful look of Cousin Herbert.
CORA. Do you think we're beginning to imagine things? I must confess that when I looked at that baby just now . . .
WALTER. Oh, no, dear. That would hardly be likely.
CORA. Truly Walter, I swear——
WALTER. Dearest, it was twenty years ago.
CORA (*weeping*) Don't.

"SHOPPING IN KENSINGTON"   No. 15

CORA (*singing*)
   Oh, Walter!
   I'm sure you've no intention
   Of hurting me
   I beg you not to mention
   That terrible day.

WALTER (*singing*)	Oh, Cora!
	We oughtn't to suppress it
	It's eating us
	It's better to express it
	Hurt us as it may.
CORA.	Very well, Walter
	Whatever you say.
BOTH.	We were shopping in Kensington
	Twenty years ago
	It was at Christmas-time
	Kensington looked so pretty in the snow
	We bought our presents there
	And it was such fun
	We found everything we wanted
	But we lost our baby son.
	He was sitting outside in his pram
	As we chose the Christmas ham
	But when we came out
	He was nowhere about
CORA.	And I said "Bother!"
WALTER.	And I said "Damn!"
BOTH.	Blow, blow thou winter wind
	Blow thou every day
	And blow Kensington to pieces
	For it snatched our babe away
	Oh that Christmas of sorrow
	The lights on the tree were dim
	The tears we've spent
	Since the day we went
	Shopping in Kensington with—him.

(*They mime rocking a baby in its pram, making funny faces at it.* CORA *goes to tuck it up but—it isn't there. They look at one another in despair*)

	Shopping in Kensington
	That was our mistake
CORA.	Who took my baby boy?
WALTER.	Babies are such silly things to take.
BOTH.	We were so occupied
	Emptying the shelves
	Of toys suitable for baby
	But we kept the toys ourselves.
WALTER.	On the mantelpiece in our home
	Is his beautiful clockwork gnome
CORA.	We've preserved with care
	The comb for his hair
WALTER.	Not that he had any hair to comb.
CORA.	Maybe he's bigger now

WALTER. That he might well be
BOTH. But if ever we should find him
We will bounce him on our knee
And say, "Baby, we're sorry"
But loss can be turned to gain
And now we know
We must never go
Shopping in Kensington again.

(*If necessary, towards the end of this number the* RUNNING TABS *can* CLOSE *behind Cora and Walter to facilitate the scene change*.)
As CORA *and* WALTER *end the song, they exit* L, *and the* LIGHTS *dim to* BLACK-OUT. *The* TANCRED EXTERIOR *cloth flies away and the* AUTHOR'S GAUZE *and* BACKING *is dropped in. The author's armchair is pushed on down* R.
OPEN RUNNING TABS (*see note above*)

SCENE 4

The scene is the Author's Flat. A SPOTLIGHT *shows* VICTORIA *sitting in the armchair, a telephone on her lap. She is in her modern costume.*

VICTORIA (*dialling a number and speaking into the receiver*) Hullo? Blanche? Victoria . . . Can I speak to Mama? I mean Mother—Mummy? . . . Guests? You mean to say they're still there? . . . Why on earth should she be frantic? . . . Well, you'd better get her. (*While she waits she sings a few bars of "Don't Make a Song and Dance About It" under her breath*) Mama? (*She rises*) I mean Mother—Mummy? I . . . I . . . I'm with Tom . . . he *isn't* scruffy . . . (*She is trying to get a word in*) What, come now?

(TOM *enters* L *and crosses to her. He carries the plastic cups which he has refilled with beer, and has a cigarette in his mouth*)

(*Shrugging her shoulders at Tom to indicate that trouble is brewing on the other end of the line*) All right, dear. . . . All right. . . . (*Suddenly bad-tempered*) All right! . . . Yes, dear. (*She rings off and puts the telephone on the seat of the armchair*) Sorry, Tom, I'll have to go. (*She collects her coat and scarf from the back of the armchair and crosses* C)
TOM (*sitting on the* L *arm of the armchair*) Oh, no!
VICTORIA. Only for a moment . . .
TOM. Can't you run away for good?
VICTORIA (*putting on coat and scarf*) Don't be silly, darling. Mother's beside herself. If I pop in and say a polite word it'll placate the guests. It'll get rid of them too. (*She crosses to Tom*)

(*Behind the gauze the* BACKING FLIES AWAY)

(*She takes the cigarette out of his mouth, kisses him, and puts the cigarette back*) I'll take a taxi. (*She crosses to* L)
TOM. What? At *this* time?

VICTORIA. Well, it may be quicker by train. I'll see.
TOM. It's the rush hour, you know. I wish you joy of it.

(*The* SPOTLIGHT *on the armchair snaps out.* TOM *exits* R *and the armchair is removed.*
    Behind the gauze the LIGHTING *snaps up to full to reveal the* TRANSPORT DROP-CLOTH, *hung at about half stage depth. This is a revue-type cloth, evocative rather than representational, and is brightly painted*)

VICTORIA. All right, I'll take a bus!

(*In the area between the gauze and the Transport Cloth, a* BUSMAN *leaps on* R)

"TAKEN FOR A RIDE"   No. 16

BUSMAN.   Going somewhere?
VICTORIA (*crossing* C)
            Oh, yes, I am. I'm going—

(*A* TRAINMAN *leaps on* L, *between the gauze and the Transport Cloth*)

TRAINMAN.   Taking a trip?
VICTORIA (*turning to face him*)
            Yes, please. I'm trying to get to—

(*A* TUBEMAN *leaps on* R *and stands up* L *of the Busman*)

TUBEMAN.   Business or pleasure?
VICTORIA (*turning to him*)
            Well, neither actually—

(*A* TAXIMAN *leaps on* L *and stands up* R *of the Trainman*)

TAXIMAN.   Is your journey really necessary?
VICTORIA (*turning to him*)
            Indeed it is! *Very* necessary!
ALL FOUR TRANSPORT OFFICIALS.
            Travel by London Transport
            And travel the luxury way!
BUSMAN.   Ting-ting!
TRAINMAN.   Hoo-hoo!
TUBEMAN.   Mind the doors!
TAXIMAN.   Jump in, lady!

(*The* AUTHOR'S FLAT GAUZE FLIES AWAY)

BUSMAN.   Take a bus.
TRAINMAN.   Take a train.
TUBEMAN.   Take a tube.
TAXIMAN.   Take a taxi.
ALL FOUR.   Trust uncle and you'll be taken for a ride.

(*The* TRANSPORT OFFICIALS *move down to join Victoria and the number proceeds*)

BUSMAN.	Travel by bus.
	And you won't travel at all.
	You'll simply stand in a queue
	For an hour or two
ALL.	You'll be there for ages.
BUSMAN.	We like holding the buses back
	Until morale begins to crack,
	Then when you are on your knees
	Along we come like a swarm of bees.
	Up you run, but before you're on
	It's "Hold very tight there" and off we've gone.
ALL	And there won't be another.
BUSMAN (*spoken*)	Jingle bells, jingle bells
	Give your legs a rest.
	Sorry, dear, we don't stop here
	It's only a Request.
TRAINMAN (*singing*)	Travel by train.
	They say it's cheaper by rail.
	But that's not the way things are
	In the restaurant car.
ALL.	Is it worth the money?
TRAINMAN.	Would you care for the brown potage?
	Oh, I've ruined your corsage!
	Try the beef, tough as teak,
	What you left on the plate last week.
	Don't you fancy the Cheddar much?
	Why not swop for the dear old Dutch?
ALL.	Try a radish with it.
TRAINMAN (*spoken*)	Where are you going to my pretty maid?
	There's a teeny delay on the line, I'm afraid.
	The driver has to stop and smoke
	For forty-five minutes at Royal Oak.
BUSMAN.	Ting-ting!
TRAINMAN.	Hoo-hoo!
TUBEMAN.	Mind the doors!
TAXIMAN.	Jump in, lady!
ALL (*singing*)	Take a bus
	Take a train
	Take a tube
	Take a taxi
	Trust uncle and you'll be taken for a ride.
TUBEMAN.	Travel by tube
	And get away from it all.
	You'll feel so safe and sound
	In the underground.
VICTORIA.	Oh, the claustrophobia!
TUBEMAN.	When you emerge, you're a limp wet rag.
	Somebody pinched your glossy mag.

	Somebody pinched your handbag too,
	And as for your bottom, it's black and blue.
	Bring your brolly and use it when
	There's any funny business from the business men.
ALL.	In between the stations.
TUBEMAN (*spoken*)	Beauty met a dirty beast
	She wasn't worried in the least
	She said, as he gave her dress a pull
	"There is no substitute for wool!"

TAXIMAN.	Travel by cab
	Ring TER 6444
	And then away we'll scoot
	By the longest route.
ALL.	See the parks of London!
TAXIMAN.	I've got a nice new meter here
	They've all been changed so it isn't clear
	What the fare should really be,
	So what you pay depends on me.
	Sixpence added for each suitcase
	And another two bob if I hate your face.
ALL.	Don't forget to tip him!
VICTORIA (*spoken*)	Taximan, Taximan, where have you been?
TAXIMAN (*spoken*)	I've been to the Strand via Golders Green.
VICTORIA.	Taximan, Taximan, what did you there?
TAXIMAN.	I piled on the extras and doubled the fare.
BUSMAN (*spoken*)	Ting, ting!
TRAINMAN (*spoken*	Hoo-hoo!
TUBEMAN (*spoken*)	Mind the doors!
TAXIMAN.	Jump in, lady!
ALL (*singing*)	Take a bus!
	Take a train!
	Take a tube!
	Take a taxi!
	Trust uncle and you'll be taken for a—

(*An* AIR HOSTESS *enters down* L)

AIR HOSTESS (*spoken*)	Why not fly B.E.A.? (*She exits down* L)
ALL.	Trust uncle and you'll be taken for a
	Nice long ride!

As the number ends the LIGHTS BLACK-OUT *and the* RUNNING TABS CLOSE.

SCENE 5

The scene is Streets of London. It is evening. A bench has been set at an angle, R.

When the LIGHTS *come up,* TOM, *dressed as a policeman, enters* L *and crosses towards the bench.*

TOM. I've lost touch with the criminals completely. (*He takes from his pocket the sketches Walter gave him in Battersea Park, and examines them*) Tancred, Wilberforce—(*he sits on the bench* R) let them go! And the hundred pounds reward with them! (*He puts the sketches away again*) I'd give more than that to set eyes on her again. (*He takes off his helmet, places it on the bench, and relaxes*) I saw her once as she ran past. I saw her again—and our eyes met. There *must* be a third time.

"LOVELY MEETING YOU AT LAST"   No. 17

TOM (*singing*) We've smiled in the street
But never seem to meet
I was always taught
Journeys ought
To end in lovers meeting.
(*He rises and strolls to* C)
I saw her today
I trembled as she passed
I'd so love to say
"Lovely meeting you at last."
(*He crosses down* L)
We should have met
Long ago
And I know
I'm a fool
I could at least have tried
(*He returns to* C)
Nothing's complete
Till we meet
You can't beat
That old rule
It mustn't be denied
(*Crossing* R, *to the bench*)
Then why the delay?
Time travels pretty fast.
(*He picks up his helmet*)
We must meet today
Kiss and play
While we may
(*He crosses slowly to* L)
I'd so love to say
"Lovely meeting you at last."
(*He exits* L)

(*The* MUSIC *of Lovely Meeting You at Last continues, as the* RUNNING TABS *open*)

Scene 6

The scene is City Centre, as Act I, Scene 8. It is late at night and the lighting is dim and shadowy.

When the Running Tabs *open, the stage is empty. After a moment* Victoria *(in period costume) enters up* R, *and a* Spotlight *picks her out. She is exhausted, depressed, and weeping. She speaks over the* Music *which plays on very softly.*

Victoria *(coming down* RC) It's hopeless, hopeless! Perhaps I was wrong to run away. No, I wasn't wrong! What else could I do? *(She weeps)*

(Tom *enters up* L *and stands in the shadows, gazing at her)*

(Not noticing Tom) But where else can I go? Everyone in London is chasing me. It feels like everyone in the world.

(The Music *fades)*

Tom *(taking a pace or two towards Victoria, but still in the shadows)* It isn't everyone in the world.
Victoria. Oh—you startled me.
Tom. I'm sorry.
Victoria. How long have you been standing there?
Tom *(moving into the pool of light around Victoria, to her* L) I don't know. It's barely three hours since I saw you on the bridge, but it seems like a lifetime.
Victoria. And now you've caught me. You want to arrest me?
Tom. I want to protect you.
Victoria. With the police that's often the same thing.
Tom. Don't cry. And please stop thinking of me as a policeman.
Victoria. If you're not you've no right to speak to me.
Tom. No. But I feel I have a right. I would give all I have—*(he pauses)* but that's not much.
Victoria. You'd give all you have . . . ?
Tom. To see you smiling; to see you dancing with happiness.
Victoria. I don't think I'll ever dance again.
Tom *(easing down stage a little)* The city's quiet and we're alone. As if the world had stopped turning. *(He turns to her and holds out his arms)* Dance with me.

(As Victoria *moves into his arms the* Music *resumes, in waltz time. They dance and gradually she relaxes, her fears vanishing)*

You're smiling. You're happy?
Victoria. I'm surrounded by troubles and I've never been so happy before.
Tom. Nor I. But life is astonishing. Have you always lived here?
Victoria. Always.

Tom. And in all these years I never saw you till today. We were strangers.
Victoria. Dear stranger!
(*They stop dancing. The* Music *continues*)
Tom. Night has fallen. The sky is closer.
(*Lost in each other, they move to the bench and sit side by side*)
Victoria. It's quiet. Footsteps echo.
Tom. It seems a hundred years ago.
Victoria. What?
Tom. That I found you here crying.

(*During the following refrain,* 1st Boy *and* Girl *enter up* r, *dancing. They cross* c. 2nd Boy *enters mid* r, *searching. After a moment,* 2nd Girl *enters down* l. *They run to meet* lc, *kiss and dance.* 3rd Boy *and* Girl *enter down* r, *greet Tom and Victoria with a happy wave, and then join the other lovers. Other couples meet and dance*)

(*He sings*)
We should have met
Long ago
And I know
I'm a fool
I could at least have tried
Nothing's complete
Till we meet
You can't beat
That old rule
It mustn't be denied
Then why the delay
Time travels pretty fast
We have met today
Won't you stay
While you may?
I so love to say
"Lovely meeting you at last."

(*The* Chorus *take up the refrain and* Tom *and* Victoria *are soon deep in conversation. Every now and then* Victoria *makes a gesture to indicate that she is telling Tom all about her recent unhappy history, and he is all sympathetic understanding*)

Boys *and* Girls. We've smiled in the street
But never seem to meet
I was always taught
Journeys ought
To end in lovers meeting

I saw her (him) today
I trembled as she (he) passed
I'd so love to say
"Lovely meeting you at last"

We should have met
Long ago
And I know
I'm a fool
I could at least have tried
Nothing's complete
Till we meet
You can't beat
That old rule
It mustn't be denied—
Be denied—

(TOM *and* VICTORIA *join the other lovers*)

TOM *and* VICTORIA.
    Then why the delay?
    Time travels pretty fast
    We have met today
    Won't you stay
    While you may
    I'd love to say
EVERYBODY.   "Lovely Meeting You at Last"
    Lovely Meeting You at Last
    Lovely Meeting You at Last.

As the MUSIC *ends, the* CHORUS *must be above the Streets of London* RUNNING TABS. TOM *returns* VICTORIA *to the bench and sits on her* L, *after putting on his helmet again. The* RUNNING TABS *close behind them.*

SCENE 7

The scene is Streets of London.

TOM. I suppose I should really be getting on with my investigation. A reward of one hundred pounds has been offered for the capture of two criminals.

VICTORIA. How exciting!

TOM. It isn't only the reward; it's my duty to catch them.

VICTORIA. Then I shall help you. What are their names?

TOM. Nonsense, Victoria! It's the middle of the night. Before I do anything I shall see you home.

VICTORIA. I tell you I've run away. Father won't have me.

TOM. He will when I tell him I want to marry you.

VICTORIA. He won't. Don't you see, it can't be just anyone. It's got to be Tancred or Wilberforce.

TOM (*electrified*) It's got to be who?

VICTORIA. One of those two. I told you. Tancred or Wilberforce.

TOM. Victoria! Could there be two Tancreds and Wilberforces?

VICTORIA. Two of each, do you mean?

TOM. Yes.

VICTORIA. Heavens! I hope not!
TOM (*producing the sketches from his pocket*) Are your Tancred and Wilberforce anything like this?
VICTORIA. That *is* them. It's them! Tom! Are these your criminals?
TOM. Yes.
VICTORIA (*rising excitedly and moving to* C) Hurray! They're criminals! I always suspected it.
TOM. Now your father *can't* make you. Now I *can* take you home.
VICTORIA. No, no! Don't you see? Now I *can* help you to catch them. They're looking for me! If I let them find me, you can arrest them!
TOM (*shocked*) Victoria! (*He moves to her,* C)
VICTORIA. Yes, yes! I can hang about in some conspicuous place, say Leicester Square, and as soon as they appear you can grab them!
TOM. To use you as a decoy like that! I wouldn't hear of it.
VICTORIA. Don't be silly, Tom! You'll be there to protect me.
TOM. Yes, of course! But if they see me, they won't come near.
VICTORIA. You can hide, can't you?
TOM. Yes.
VICTORIA. Then leap out at the appropriate moment.
TOM. Yes, yes.
VICTORIA. Now—(*pointing* L) hide there! (*Changing her mind and pointing* R) No, there! I'll whistle when I see them. (*She rushes Tom to* R)

(TOM *exits* R, *and removes his helmet and jacket*)

(*Coming well* L *of centre*) Now! How do I make myself conspicuous?

(*Except for a* SPOTLIGHT *on Victoria, all lights* DIM *to* OUT. *Under cover of the darkness, the bench* R *is struck*)

(*She calls out*) Mr Tancred! Mr Wilberforce! Oooo-ooh! There isn't a sound or sight of them. The town might be empty. (*She moves a little further* L) Nothing but silence. . . . Silence. . . . Silence. (*She freezes*)

(*After a pause* TOM, *as the author, enters* R. *A second* SPOTLIGHT *picks him out*)

TOM. And so Victoria waited alone in the empty street. She was no longer tired, no longer forlorn. Minutes passed and she didn't mind. Hours passed and she scarcely noticed them. She had no fear that her pursuers would not find her. She felt herself encircled in a blaze of light. . . . Then far, far away, far in the distance, she thought she heard a faint sound that might have been footsteps.

REPRISE—"THE LONG CHASE" No. 18

(*The* CHASE MUSIC *creeps in, very softly. From this point on* VICTORIA *comes to life again and reacts to the author's words*)

It was scarcely a sound. She might have imagined it. She shook herself and listened again, straining her ears. Yes, it was there!

(*The* MUSIC *begins to crescendo*)

It must be they! It must be! They came nearer and nearer. She could barely contain herself. She began to dance up and down, to mark time dancing. Soon she would see them. They were coming that way—no, *that* way. The sound filled her ears. It echoed through the streets. It filled the city. It must wake everyone. Louder and louder! Nearer and nearer! It came from every direction . . .

(*Perhaps the author had more to say, but we shall never know for now the* MUSIC *drowns his voice. Suddenly* VICTORIA *tries excitedly to whistle. She cannot. She puts her fingers in her mouth and tries, and fails, again. She takes fright and runs to* L)

VICTORIA (*shrieking back over her shoulder*) Tom! Tom! (*She exits* L)

(TOM *runs after her and exits* L. *The* MUSIC *is now fortissimo and the* LIGHTS *begin to build slightly, but still dim and sinister. The* CHASE *arrives from* R. *With the exception of* MR *and* MRS GILCHRIST *they are all there:* TANCRED *and* WILBERFORCE, MISS PAYTON, WALTER *and* CORA, EFFIE *and* EDWARD, *some of the* SHOPPERS, BY-STANDERS *and* PASSERS-BY, *even the* LOVERS, *but now they are figures in a nightmare, grim and determined, crossing menacingly from* R *to* L. *Lastly, the* YOUNG MOTHER *hurries on, still pushing her pram. The* BABY *is crying so loudly it can be heard even above the music. She stops* C *and glares into the pram*)

YOUNG MOTHER (*timed to coincide with the end of the music*) Oh, shut up!

Instantly there is silence, not only from the Baby, but also from the Orchestra. *The* YOUNG MOTHER *turns to the audience and gives a big, beaming smile of triumph. The* LIGHTS BLACK-OUT.

Under cover of darkness the YOUNG MOTHER *exits and the* RUNNING TABS *open.*

SCENE 8

The scene is the Drawing-room of the Gilchrists' House, as it was in Act I, Scene 2, when the stagehands had finished dressing it, except that a second chair, matching the one used earlier by Tancred, which is still up C, *replaces the long stool below the piano*, RC. *The long stool is now set at an angle across* L, *and has a cushion on the downstage end of it. The flowers on the pedestal have been replaced by a splendid aspidistra.*

When the LIGHTS *come up*, MR GILCHRIST *stands to the* R *of the chair below the piano*, RC, *and* MRS GILCHRIST *stands to the* L *of the chair up* C. *Each holds an open copy of a large operatic score which they are studying.*

MRS GILCHRIST (*lifting her head from the score and addressing the audience*) Mr and Mrs Gilchrist, having abandoned the chase through age and exhaustion——

MR GILCHRIST (*looking up from his score, to the audience*) —withdrew to their withdrawing-room where they restlessly thumbed through their music cabinet.

MRS GILCHRIST. As Mr Gilchrist remarked . . .
MR GILCHRIST (*to Mrs Gilchrist*) When you're in despair, there's nothing like a bit of singing for expressing it.
MRS GILCHRIST (*still to the audience*) Not in vain were they members of the Battersea Choral Society, and they had done their bit of rehearsing. (*She sits on the chair up* C)
MR GILCHRIST. You know where to come in, Biddy? I sing my bit, and then you sing your bit. Right?
MRS GILCHRIST. Right.

(MR GILCHRIST *poses in the approved fashion with the open score, and clears his throat. He glances once more at his wife and* MRS GILCHRIST *nods graciously to indicate that she is ready to start. The introduction to* "*Waiting For Our Daughter*" *begins*)

"WAITING FOR OUR DAUGHTER" No. 19

MR GILCHRIST (*singing*)
>While we're waiting for our daughter
>All the world is standing still
>Every moment seems eternal
>These are hours we cannot kill.
>We have swept and we have dusted
>We have played an indoor game
>But the clock has not moved forward
>Both its hands have stayed the same.

(*He almost closes his score and moves down* RC. MRS GILCHRIST *thinks he has finished, rises, moves down to his* L *and takes a big breath to start singing.* MR GILCHRIST, *at that moment, opens his score again and presses on*)

>While we're waiting for our daughter

(MRS GILCHRIST *recognizes her mistake and tiptoes back up* C *to her chair. She sits, shamefacedly*)

>What is left for us to do?
>We have talked and we have argued
>We have shed a tear or two

(MRS GILCHRIST *wonders if this is her cue and hesitantly looks up again. A black glance from* MR GILCHRIST *puts her head sharply back into her score*)

>We have washed and dried the dishes
>After two resplendent meals.
>Our larder and our hearts are empty
>Only *we* know how it feels

(MRS GILCHRIST *feels certain this is it, and sweeps down to his* L. *Unfortunately, as she gets there,* MR GILCHRIST *sings on. Without pause she wheels* L *to return to her chair, but* MR GILCHRIST *strikes a new attitude and accidently places his* L *foot firmly on the train of her dress and escape is impossible*)

> While we're waiting for our daughter
> What is left for us to say?
> We've exhausted conversation
> And our minds are far away.

(MRS GILCHRIST *is still struggling*)

> Stars have passed upon the zenith
> Earth and moon are standing still

(*He again alters his pose, allowing* MRS GILCHRIST *to trip to* L. *She sits on the long low stool and nonchalantly pats the cushion to her* L, *which leaks a few feathers*)

> Every moment seems eternal
> These are hours we cannot kill

(*He has finished and turns away to take his place on the chair* R. MRS GILCHRIST *realizes there is silence and hurries to* C. *Before she can begin to sing, however, she must remove a feather which has found its way into her mouth. At last she nods that she is ready, and the* MUSIC *continues with a long Handelian introduction*)

MRS GILCHRIST (*at last; in recitative*)
    My daughter . . .
    (*She turns a page and the introduction plods interminably on*)
    My daughter . . . has gone . . . run away . . .
    (*She measures out the beats of the music with vigorous nods of the head*)
    Vanished . . .
    She left her chamber . . .
    (*Unable to believe that she has read the last phrase correctly, she peers closely at the score. Reassured, she sings on*)
    She left her chamber . . . and disappeared,
    And disappeared into the unfriendly night . . .
    We cannot organize a methodical search owing to our reduced
        financial circumstances. . . .
    (*She runs out of breath and staggers downstage a couple of paces, exhausted*)
    How can we hope when the night is wild?
    How can we hope for a fortune so fair?
    To catch the flee—
    To catch the flee——
    To catch the fleeting child?
    I'll lay me down and sleep with—
    (*Apprehensively, she turns a page; then, relieved*)
                               —despair.
    I'll lay me down—
    (*Crossing to the stool* L *and plumping up the cushion*)
                  —and sleep with despair.
    (*She does her best to make herself comfortable on the long stool, lying face down, her head on the cushion*)

(MR GILCHRIST *rises and moves to* C, *where he reopens his score and sings from it*)

MR GILCHRIST (*unexpectedly*)
Toreador now guard thee!
Toreador! Toreador!
(*He pauses, examines the score, removes a loose page which he discards, and continues, happier*)
Oh rise and take heart for the sum of our sorrow
(*He turns a page*)
Will be cancelled and paid by the dawn of tomorrow
Oh strengthen your soul or the gods will forsake us
If we do not falter then nothing can make us.
(*He crosses* L *to above the long stool*)
Oh rise—

(MRS GILCHRIST *lifts her posterior and* MR GILCHRIST *balances his score on it*)

—and take heart I command it,
Oh strengthen your soul, I demand it.

(MRS GILCHRIST *subsides.* MR GILCHRIST *catches his score just in time.* MRS GILCHRIST *swivels round and sits on the* L *of the stool.* MR GILCHRIST *sits to her* R *and takes her* R *hand in his* L *hand. They have their scores on their laps and, with their free hands, open and shut them with each of the following phrases*)

MRS GILCHRIST. I cannot.
MR GILCHRIST. You can.
MRS GILCHRIST. I dare not.
MR GILCHRIST. You dare.
MRS GILCHRIST. I may not.
MR GILCHRIST. You may.
MRS GILCHRIST. I must not.
MR GILCHRIST (*losing his temper and throwing her hand free*)
You must!
MRS GILCHRIST. No.
MR GILCHRIST. Yes. (*He stands*)
MRS GILCHRIST. No, no.
MR GILCHRIST (*offering his hand to help her to rise*)
Yes, yes.
MRS GILCHRIST (*getting shakily to her feet*)
I faint.
MR GILCHRIST. No, no, no!
MRS GILCHRIST. I fail.
MR GILCHRIST. No, no, no, no!
MRS GILCHRIST. I'm dying.

(*They pause, each convinced that the other has to sing next. Each turns a page, and* MR GILCHRIST *offers a guilty smile of apology before going into his* CADENZA)

Mr Gilchrist (*taking his* Cadenza)
Ah . . . !
Both.   We will go and chase our daughter,
We will dare the deep of night.
We will run with steps unfailing
Till we have her in our sight.
We will then exchange forgiveness
All our former sins erase

(Mr Gilchrist *shuts his score and puts a comforting arm around Mrs Gilchrist*)
And live happy ever after
All our sunlit future days.

(*They finish with a prolonged* Cadenza)
Ah . . . !

(*They bow to each other in the manner of concert artists acknowledging applause. The* Lights *begin to dim*)

Mr Gilchrist (*leading her* R) Come, Biddy. Everything will seem brighter in the morning.

(*As they retire, the* Lights *dim to* Black-Out. *There is a slight pause to indicate the passing of time.*
A faint glimmer of Light *returns and we can just make out that someone has entered up* L)

Tom (*calling from off up* L, *in the darkness*) Victoria! Victoria!
Victoria (*gently, from close at hand*) It's all right. I'm here.

(*The* Lights *build a little.* Victoria *is moving from* C *stage to down* L. Tom *enters from up* L *and moves to up* C. *He is dressed as the policeman*)

Tom. Where are we?
Victoria. Wait. I'll find a light.

(*The* Lights *snap up to* Full)

There! (*A little breathless*) This is my house.
Tom (*crossing to the piano, up* R) Your house! Did you *mean* to come here?
Victoria. Yes. They'd be sure to finish up here. (*She crosses up* C) They've been making themselves at home here for years. But where *are* they, Tom? (*Peering anxiously off up* L) I thought they were just behind me.
Tom (*wandering round and appraising the room with interest*) I overtook them.
Victoria. You shouldn't have done that; they *must* catch me!
Tom (*moving up* L *and examining the aspidistra*) So this is where you live. (*He strokes an aspidistra leaf*) Very contemporary.
Victoria (*crossing to him*) Tom, you let them lose me.
Tom (*turning and embracing her*) Don't worry. They must have seen us come in.

(*The* Chase Music *begins quietly*)

REPRISE—"THE END OF THE CHASE"   No. 20

VICTORIA. Listen! Footsteps!
TOM. It's them!
VICTORIA (*moving down* R) Quick, hide!

(TOM *ducks down, hiding below the aspidistra, as* TANCRED *and* WILBERFORCE, *carrying their picture between them, enter up* L *above the aspidistra.* TANCRED *and* WILBERFORCE *cross* R *to the piano and* TOM *stealthily moves round to the* L *of, and then above the aspidistra*)

TANCRED
WILBERFORCE } (*spotting Victoria together*) Victoria!

(*They prop the picture against the piano, its back to the audience, and close on Victoria down stage.* VICTORIA *eases to* RC)

WILBERFORCE (*closing to Victoria's* R) I said it first.
TANCRED (*to Victoria's* L) You didn't.
WILBERFORCE. I did.

(TOM *emerges quickly from hiding, moves between Victoria and Tancred, and places the heavy hand of the law on Tancred's* R *shoulder and Wilberforce's* L *shoulder.* TANCRED *and* WILBERFORCE *squeal in panic and start to wriggle*)

VICTORIA (*moving round* R *of Wilberforce*) Oh, Tom, what shall we do? Oh *keep still!*

(*The group struggles to up* C)

TOM. Blow my whistle. The effect should be instantaneous.

(VICTORIA *crosses to Tom and yanks the lanyard on which Tom's whistle hangs in his pocket. She blows a piercing blast before moving back to* RC. TANCRED *and* WILBERFORCE *stop struggling and cover their ears*)

TANCRED. Victoria!
WILBERFORCE. Victoria!

(*At once* MR GILCHRIST, *in nightshirt and tasselled cap, and* MRS GILCHRIST, *in dressing-gown and mob-cap, enter down* R. WALTER *and* CORA *pound on down* L, *and all other members of the* CHASE *rush on up* L)

MR GILCHRIST. Victoria!
MRS GILCHRIST. Victoria, at last!

(MR *and* MRS GILCHRIST *are down* R, VICTORIA RC, WILBERFORCE *and* TANCRED *up* C *with* TOM, CORA *and* WALTER *down* L. *The rest of the company are grouped up* R *above and around the piano, up* L *above and around the aspidistra, and down* L *behind the Miskins*)

REPRISE—"VICTORIA, VICTORIA!"   No. 21

ALL.   Oh, now we've found Victoria
Victoria, Victoria,
We're dancing round and joys abound
And never more we'll part.

For here is our Victoria
Victoria, Victoria,
Our lovely erring daughter and
Our own sweetheart.

(*As the* REPRISE *ends,* WALTER *recognizes Tancred and Wilberforce and moves threateningly towards them, up* C)

WALTER (*thunderously*) These are the men who stole my picture!
MR GILCHRIST. Excuse me, sir. This is my house.
WALTER (*turning back down* L) Well, it's nothing to boast about.

(MR *and* MRS GILCHRIST *are shocked*)

(*He faces Tancred and Wilberforce again*) Where's my picture?

(*A* YOUNG MAN *in the group by the piano finds the picture and brings it* C *to Wilberforce and Tancred, who hold it between them, its back to the audience*)

WILBERFORCE. Here, sir.
TANCRED. We've improved it.
WILBERFORCE. We've increased its value.

(*They circle round so that the portrait itself can be seen for the first time. Across it in bold type are the words* "WILBERTAN BABY SOAP")

ALL (*shocked at the vandalism*) Oh!

(TANCRED *produces a bar of soap from his pocket and he and* WILBERFORCE *place it on the portrait so that the baby appears to be holding it*)

WALTER. You've destroyed my masterpiece!
TANCRED. Destroyed it? No!
WILBERFORCE. We've used it. Art in the service of industry.
TANCRED. Industry in the service of art. A great picture on every wrapper.
WILBERFORCE. Mutual advertising.

(*Holding the picture under their chins they sing;* TANCRED R, WILBERFORCE L)

"THE SOAP COMMERCIAL" No. 22

TANCRED *and* WILBERFORCE.
        Baby's as pretty as a picture,
ALL.   With Wilbertan, Wilbertan.
TANCRED *and* WILBERFORCE.
        If ever a baby has charms he's got 'em
        What is it makes his cheeks so red?
        A soap as soft as a baby's bottom,
        Baby uses—
ALL.   —Wilbertan.
TANCRED *and* WILBERFORCE.
        Preparing to be a beautiful man!
        Baby's beautiful.

(WALTER *can stand no more and moves up* C. *He grabs the picture*)

WALTER. Gibbering lunatics! (*He takes the picture back to Cora*)
CORA. Hang them!
MRS GILCHRIST. Excuse me, this is my house.
WALTER (*testily*) Then why don't you offer me a drink?

(CORA *and* WALTER *examine the picture in sorrow, down* L)

TOM (*returning to arrest Tancred and Wilberforce*) Come along quietly now. (*He stands between them and addresses Walter*) What is the charge, sir?
WALTER. Oh, I don't charge them. This picture can be restored.
TOM (*to Mr Gilchrist*) And you, sir?
MR GILCHRIST. Oh, *I* don't charge them, if they lay off my daughter.
TOM. Victoria?
VICTORIA (*crossing to* R *of Tancred*) Oh, let them go. They're guilty but insane.

(TOM *releases Tancred and Wilberforce and crosses down* L *to Walter*)

TOM. Sir, excuse me, but a little matter of a hundred pounds reward.
WALTER. What? Oh, yes, certainly. Cora, have you any money?
CORA. Well, not on me.
WALTER. There may be some in my other suit. Perhaps we could post it. Who are you, sir?
TOM. I'm the subject of this picture.
EVERYONE. The son!
WALTER. You?
CORA (*rushing to embrace him*) My son!
WALTER. Now, don't be hasty! He must prove it you know.
TOM. I remember sitting for it—and how I hated playing with that beastly pipe.
CORA. Oh, would you mind taking up your pose—just so that we can . . .

(TOM *moves up* C, *adopting the pose of the portrait; a child playing with a bubble-pipe*)

It is! It is! (*She crosses to Tom's* R) My son!
ALL. Ah!!
TOM (*rising*) Mother! (*He kisses Cora*)

(WALTER *moves up, arms extended*)

Father! (*He kisses Walter*) May I present my future wife?

(VICTORIA *closes in to Cora's* R *and shakes hands with her*)

CORA. Charming! Haven't we met before, somewhere?
VICTORIA. Yes. (*She turns to down* R) Papa, may I present my future husband? (*She brings* TOM *down* C)
MR GILCHRIST (*coming to* R *of Victoria*) Not so fast! What are your qualifications, young man?
TOM. Qualifications?

MR GILCHRIST. Who are you, and what have you?
TOM. I am Tom Miskin, Esquire.
MR GILCHRIST. And what have you?
TOM. I have two pounds a week.
MR GILCHRIST. Not enough.
TOM. A tender heart.
MR GILCHRIST. Not enough.
TOM. And—oh, yes, I have a reward of one hundred pounds.
MR GILCHRIST. Enough. (*He turns away down* L)
MRS GILCHRIST (*crossing to kiss Victoria*) Bless you, my children.
(*She moves to Mr Gilchrist's* L)
TOM (*turning to Victoria*) Dear stranger.
VICTORIA. Dear friend.

(*The* LIGHTS *indicate that this is the dawn of a lovely new day as the* COMPANY *sing*)

REPRISE "LOVELY MEETING YOU'" No. 23

ALL.
We should have met
Long ago
And I know
I'm a fool
I could at least have tried
Nothing's complete
Till we meet
You can't beat
That old rule
It mustn't be denied

(*The* COMPANY *begin to drift away as* TOM *and* VICTORIA *move down* C *together*)

Then why the delay?
Time travels pretty fast.
Now you've met today
Kiss and play
While you may

(TOM *and* VICTORIA *are alone*)

TOM *and* VICTORIA.
I so love to say
"Lovely meeting you at last."

(*The* AUTHOR'S FLAT GAUZE *drops in, then the* BACKING)

VICTORIA. Well, that's it! (*She starts to unpin her curls*) And they all lived happily ever after!
TOM (*taking off his helmet*) Of course.
VICTORIA. Of course. Except I bet you never got that hundred pounds.
TOM. From Walter Miskin?

VICTORIA. Walter Miskin hasn't got a bean.
TOM. Well, I always knew that. (*He starts to unbutton his tunic*)
VICTORIA. *I'd* marry you *without* a hundred pounds.
TOM. You would?
VICTORIA (*tenderly*) I *will* marry you without a hundred pounds.
TOM (*for a moment delighted and surprised, then doing his best to take it all in his stride*) And if your father still doesn't like my hair style?
VICTORIA. Then I'll defy him and run away.

(TOM *kisses her*)

Tom, I *must* go home!
TOM. No! You're always going home. Why?
VICTORIA. It's terribly late. I might as well humour them till I *do* run away.
TOM (*consenting and protective*) All right. I'll see you to your door.
VICTORIA. It's a long way.
TOM. Shall I call a cab?
VICTORIA. No, let's walk. It's nicer.
TOM. And takes longer.

The Streets of London RUNNING TABS *close.* MUSIC *begins.*

SCENE 9

"EVENING IN LONDON" No. 24

TOM *and* VICTORIA (*singing*)
    Evening in London
    And homeward we stray
    Strolling so slowly
    To lengthen the way.
    (*They move slowly towards* L)
    Seeking the shadows,
    Avoiding the light,
    Always postponing
    The time to say good night. . . .

(*As they exit* L *the* RUNNING TABS *open*)

The scene is City Centre, but it is gayer and more colourful than earlier in the show. The STARS *are out and the* STREET-LAMPS *are bright. The* COCKNEYS *are there, and the rest of the* COMPANY *stroll as they sing the* FINALE. *During the song all the* PRINCIPALS *return to take their* CURTAIN CALLS.

ALL.   Evening in London
      The city's at rest
      Evening in London
      The sky's at its best
      Lovers are sighing

And dancers arrive
Daylight is dying
And theatres come alive.

Cabmen are cruising
To pick up a fare
Ladies are choosing
What jewels to wear
Flowers and ribbons
To flatter a gown
On a summer evening
In London town.

The gentry are dining
The windows are shining
Ablaze with a million lights.
The Bow Bells are pealing
And we have a feeling
Tonight will be one of those
Wonderful nights.

Evening in London
The street-lamps aglow
Evening in London
And homeward we go.
Shadows are falling,
The sun's going down
On a summer evening
In London town.

(*An extra blaze of* LIGHT *welcomes the return of* TOM *and* VICTORIA)

Evening in London
The street-lamps aglow
Evening in London
And homeward we go.
Shadows are falling,
The sun's going down
On a summer evening
In London town.

The CURTAIN *falls.*

CURTAIN CALLS   No. 1

ALL.   Let's make a song and dance about it
Let's make a row!
Something's about that's getting to scare the town!
As for convention, we shall flout it
You've shown us how!
And with a shout we're letting our hair right down!

	We are
	What you make us
	You've just
	Got to take us
	By the hand
	We've not a
	Chance without it!
	So we must make a song and dance about it
	Let's make it now! Yes, now!
	Let's make
	A song and dance!
	Song and dance,
	Song and dance!

No. 2

ALL.	Solitary stranger
	Where did you come from?
	What have you run from?
	Did you do something wrong?
	Can you be in danger?
	Let us befriend you
	Couldn't we send you
	Back to where you belong?
GIRLS.	D'you seek a lonely street
	For cover?
MEN.	Or have you flown to meet
	Your lover?
ALL.	Solitary stranger
	Are you in hiding?
	Are you deciding
	Here you will spend your days?
	And be a Solitary Stranger
	Always.

No. 3

MEN.	Follow That Girl
	I'll have to
	Follow that girl
	That girl who
	Came into my life
	From nowhere
	Now I'll have to go where-
	Ever she goes
	I'll have to
	Follow my nose
	Until the
	Day she is my wife
	I'll Follow That Girl
GIRLS.	I never
	Knew a man could fall in love
	So suddenly

MEN.	But when she
	Ran away the only thought
	That came to me
ALL.	Was, I must
	Follow That Girl
	I've got to
	Follow That Girl
	That girl is
	Definitely worth
	My ardour
	If she runs I'll run the harder
	Right across the earth
	I'll Follow That Girl
	Follow That Girl.

Final CURTAIN

FURNITURE AND PROPERTY PLOT

ACT I

Scene 1

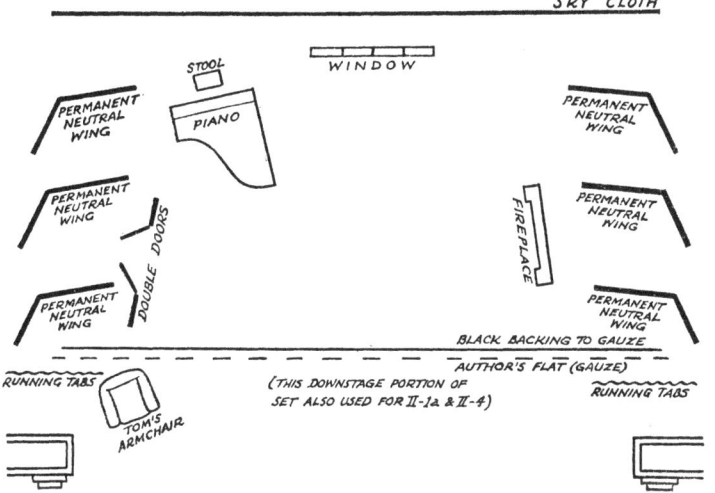

On stage: Armchair (*down* R)
          Grand piano (*up* RC) *On it:* music of a song containing several pages. *Under the lid:* a pistol (loaded 2 blank shots)
          Piano stool (above piano)

Off stage: Long low stool, down L (1ST STAGE-HAND)
          Pedestal, up L (2ND STAGE-HAND)
          Chair, up L (2ND STAGE-HAND)
          Large vase containing flowers, down R (1ST STAGE-HAND)
          Strip of carpet, down R (2ND STAGE-HAND)
          Portrait of Oscar Gilchrist, J.P., down R (2ND STAGE-HAND)

Personal: TOM: script containing loose pages, pencil
          VICTORIA: coat and scarf
          TANCRED: posy of flowers

WILBERFORCE: posy of loose flowers
MRS GILCHRIST: hairpins, Alice band, locket and chain (for Victoria)

SCENE 2

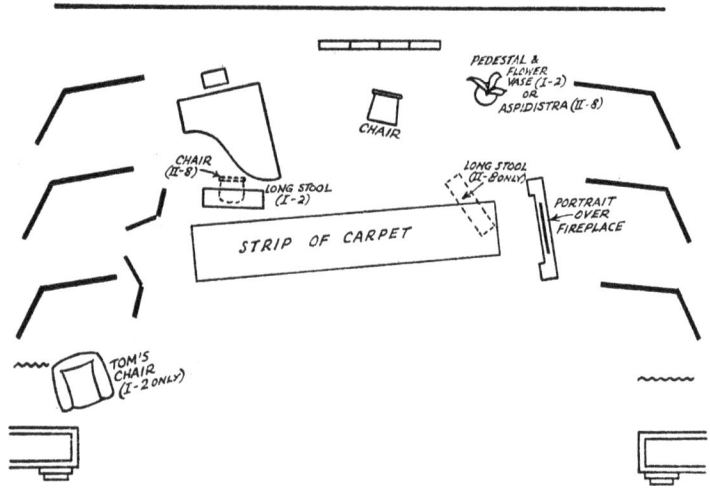

Personal: MRS GILCHRIST: Victoria's note

SCENE 3

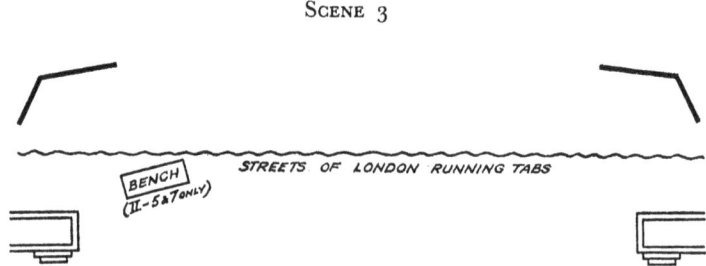

No properties

Scene 4

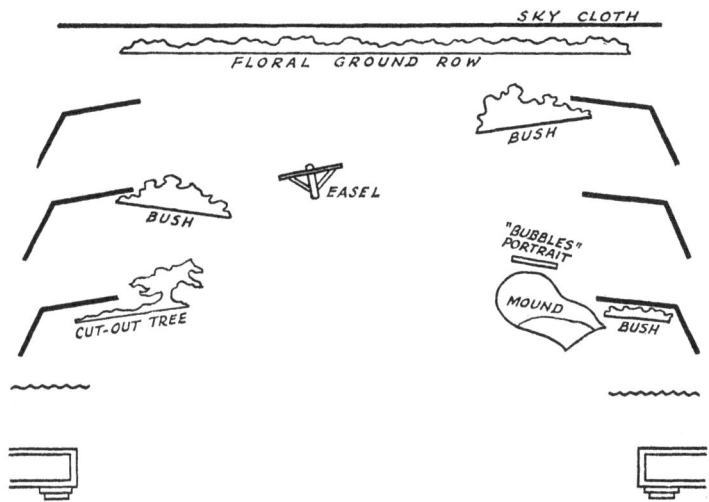

On stage: Stuffed dove, property cornucopia (by Mound, down L)
Portrait of baby in "Bubbles" pose (above mound, down L)
Artist's easel (up RC) *On it:* portrait of Cora in "Leonora and the Dove". *By it:* artist's shoulder bag, palette, oil paints, brushes, etc.

Personal: WALTER: hip flask
TOM: script, pencil
WALTER (*second entrance*): WANTED poster with portraits of Tancred and Wilberforce, hammer, nails, sketch-pad and pencil
MR GILCHRIST: Wallet containing a number of photographs

Scene 5

(*Plan as for Act I, Scene 3*)

Personal: TANCRED *and* WILBERFORCE: "Bubbles" picture from Act I, Scene 4

Scene 6

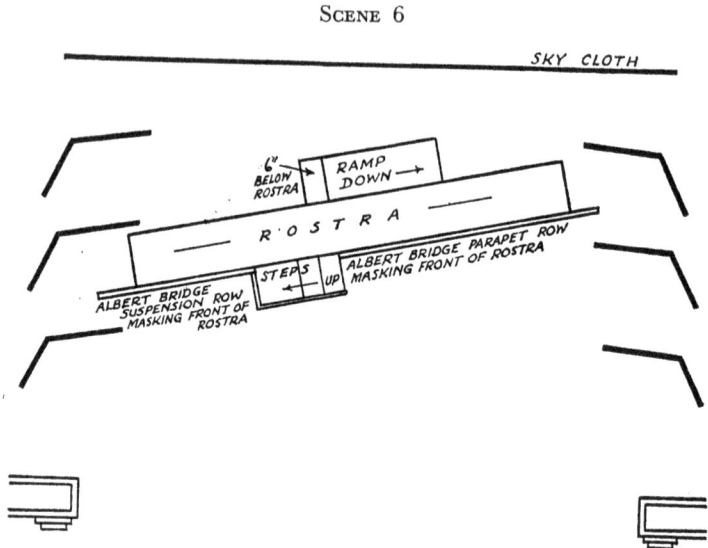

Personal: WALTER: easel, shoulder-bag and painting equipment from Act I, Scene 4, blank canvas
1ST GIRL BYSTANDER: red parasol

Scene 7

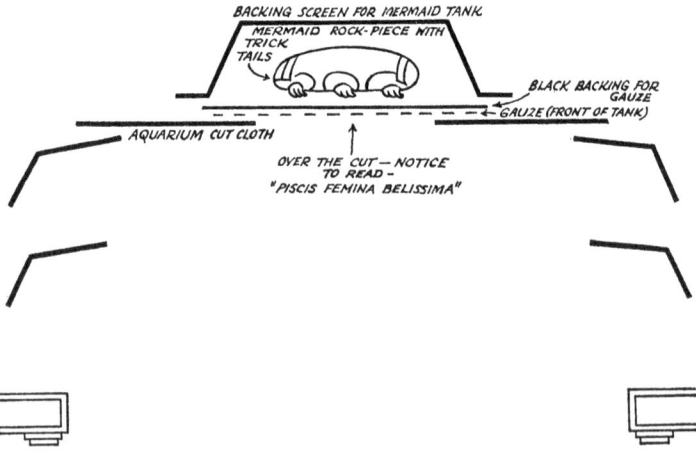

On stage: Bench (LC)

Personal: AQUARIUM KEEPER: broom
MERCIA: mirror, mascara brush
MAVIS: mirror, comb
MAUD: rouge puff

SCENE 8

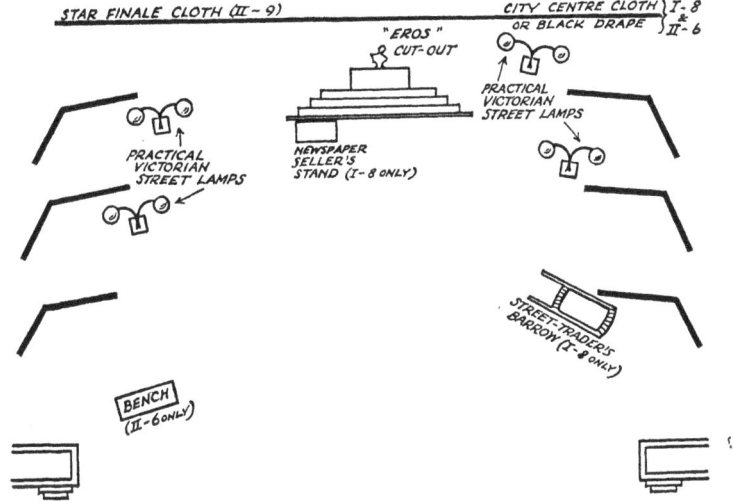

On stage (optional) Newspaper-seller's stand (up C)
Street-trader's barrow (down L)
Practical street lamps (ad lib.)

Personal: TANCRED *and* WILBERFORCE: sandwich-boards lettered "WILBER-TAN BABY SOAP"
1ST GENTLEMAN PASSER-BY: road map

ACT II

Scene 1

(Plan as for downstage portion of Act I, Scene 1)

On stage: Armchair from Act I, Scene 1 (down R) *On it:* Victoria's coat and scarf

Personal: TOM: script with loose page, plastic mug filled with beer
VICTORIA: plastic mug filled with beer
MRS GILCHRIST: handkerchief with black-trimmed edge
TANCRED *and* WILBERFORCE: handkerchiefs
2 GIRLS: parasols

Scene 2

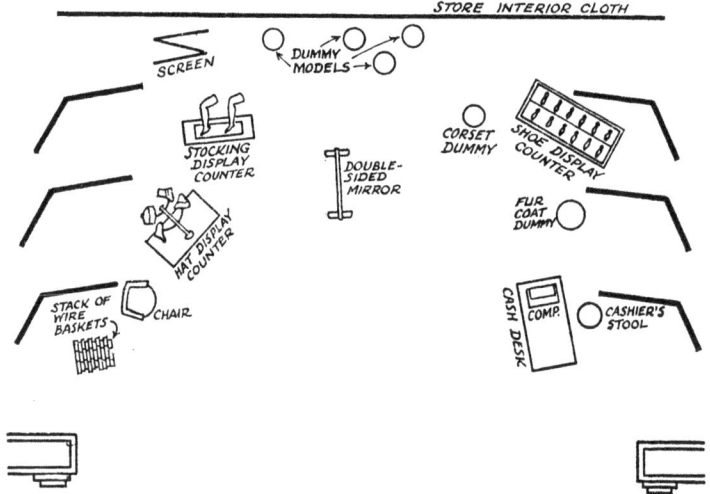

On stage: Notice to read "The Management accepts no responsibility for anything that happens in this Establishment" (on back wall)
Quantity of wire baskets (down R)
Chair with padded seat (R)
Counter displaying hats (R)
Counter displaying stocking (up R) *On it:* 2 model "legs"
Folding screen (up R) *Inside it:* loose notice on string, to read "DO NOT DISTURB"
Dummy models displaying gowns (up stage)
Double-sided mirror on stand (up C)
Dummy model displaying corset (up L)
Counter displaying shoes (L)
Dummy model displaying fur coat (mid-L)

FOLLOW THAT GIRL

        Cash-desk (down L) *On it:* trick comptometer to issue strip receipts
        Cashier's stool (behind desk)

Personal: ALL SHOPPERS: money to pay for purchases
        CUSTOMER-IN-A-HURRY: shopping basket, money
        MRS GILCHRIST: hat, umbrella, handbag
        2 DETERMINED SHOPPERS: money
        EDWARD: 2 wire baskets filled with wrapped parcels
        WALTER: money
        TANCRED *and* WILBERFORCE: black arm-bands, "Bubbles" picture from Act I, Scene 4
        LATE SHOPPER: money

SCENE 3

Personal: YOUNG MOTHER: pram

SCENE 4

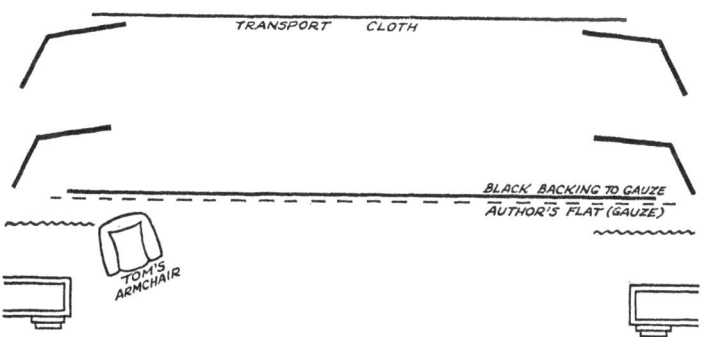

On stage: Armchair (down R) from Act I, Scene 1. *On it:* telephone. *Over back of it:* Victoria's coat and scarf

Personal: TOM: 2 plastic cups filled with beer, lit cigarette

Scene 5

(Plan as for Act I, Scene 3)

On stage: Bench (R)

Personal: TOM: sketches

Scene 6

(Plan as for Act I, Scene 8)

No properties

Scene 7

(Plan as for Act I, Scene 3)

Personal: YOUNG MOTHER: pram

Scene 8

(Plan as for Act I, Scene 2)

On stage: Grand piano (up RC) from Act I, Scene 1
Piano stool (above piano) from Act I, Scene 1
Chair (RC, below piano)
Chair (up C) from Act I, Scene 1
Pedestal (up L) from Act I, Scene 1. *On it:* aspidistra in bowl
Strip of carpet running between fireplace and double doors from Act I, Scene 1
Portrait of Gilchrist over fireplace from Act I, Scene 1
Long stool (L) from Act I, Scene 1. *On it:* cushion with feather "leak"

Personal: MR GILCHRIST: musical score with loose page
MRS GILCHRIST: musical score
TANCRED *and* WILBERFORCE: "Bubbles" picture with soap advertisement superimposed ("WILBERTAN BABY SOAP") and studs to hold bar of soap on baby's hand
WILBERFORCE: bar of soap
TOM: policeman's whistle on lanyard

Scene 9

(Plan as for Act I, Scene 8)

No properties

GENERAL LIGHTING PLOT

This basic plot assumes that three Battens are available, No. 1 to light the downstage area, No. 2 at mid-stage, No. 3 to light the backcloth, each Batten containing three circuits (pale blues and green/straws and pale yellows/rose and pinks) and all operating on dimmers. Floats, where fitted, may be used in conjunction with Batten No. 1.

One Acting Area Spot is required for the Mermaid Tank, c stage, and this should be wired independently of other circuits. Two Following Spots are required, and their Plots are printed separately.

ACT I, SCENE 1. Interior. Spring evening
To open: Batten No. 1 at ¼

Cue 1	TOM: "The whole company." *Battens No. 2 and 3 snap on at ½* *Batten No. 1 up to ½*	(Page 2)
Cue 2	VICTORIA: "The lighting shows it's day." *Battens No. 1, 2 and 3 quick build to FULL*	(Page 3)
Cue 3	Applause following opening number *Battens No. 1, 2 and 3 dim to B.O.*	(Page 4)
Cue 4	TOM: "It's a summer evening." *Battens No. 2 and 3 (not on dimmer), snap on circuits one by one to give gradual return to FULL*	(Page 4)
Cue 5	TOM exits and his armchair is moved aside *Batten No. 1 quick build to FULL*	(Page 6)

ACT I, SCENE 2. Interior. Day
To open: Battens No. 1, 2 and 3 at FULL

Cue 6	MR GILCHRIST follows the chase *Battens No. 1, 2 and 3 dim to ½*	(Page 14)
Cue 7	MRS GILCHRIST exits *Battens No. 1, 2 and 3 continue dim to B.O.*	(Page 14)

ACT I, SCENE 3 (RUNNING TABS)   (Page 14
When TABS closed: Batten No. 1 snap up to FULL

ACT I, SCENE 4. Exterior. Day   Page 15)
As RUNNING TABS open: Battens No. 2 and 3 snap up FULL

ACT I, SCENE 5 (RUNNING TABS)   (Page 24)
Batten No. 1 remains at FULL

ACT I, SCENE 6. Exterior. Early evening   (Page 25)
To open: Battens No. 1 and 2 at FULL
Batten No. 3 at ½

Cue 8	End of "Solitary Stranger" Batten No. 2 dim to ½	(Page 27)
Cue 9	TANCRED: "We're British, aren't we?" Battens 2 and 3 build to FULL	(Page 28)
Cue 10	BYSTANDERS (*singing*): "Lost, stolen or strayed." Batten No. 1 slow dim to B.O.	(Page 29)

ACT I, SCENE 7. Interior. Dimly lit
To open: No lighting

Cue 11	When RUNNING TABS open Battens No. 1 and 2, very slow build on blue/green circuits only to ½	(Page 29)
Cue 12	VICTORIA and KEEPER exit Acting Area Spot snaps ON Mermaid Tank	(Page 31)
Cue 13	MERMAIDS escape from tank Battens No. 1 and 2 snap ON remaining circuits at ½	(Page 33)
Cue 14	End of "Three Victorian Mermaids" Acting Area Spot snaps OUT	(Page 33)
Cue 15	VICTORIA and KEEPER re-enter Battens No. 1 and 2 slow build to FULL	(Page 33)
Cue 16	End of "Mermaid Scales" Battens No. 1 and 2, snap B.O.	(Page 35)

ACT I, SCENE 8. Exterior. Night
  THE APPARENT SOURCES OF LIGHT are moonlight and street lamps.
  Property fittings (optional) Victorian Street Lamps, ad lib.
To open: Battens No. 1, 2 and 3 and property fittings ON. Remain
  to end of Act

ACT II, SCENE 1. Interior. Spring evening, as Act I, Scene 1
To open: Batten No. 1 at ¼

Cue 17	MRS GILCHRIST: "Lights, please." Batten No. 1 dim to B.O.	(Page 40)
Cue 18	VICTORIA exits, and the armchair is struck Batten No. 1. Build to ½	(Page 41)
Cue 19	TOM: "push authors around." Batten No. 1 complete build to FULL	(Page 41)

ACT II, SCENE 2. Interior. Day
To open: Battens No. 1, 2 and 3 at FULL

Cue 20	End of "Follow That Girl" Reprise Battens No. 1, 2 and 3 dim to B.O.	(Page 53)

ACT II, SCENE 3. Exterior. Day
To open: Batten No. 1 at FULL

Cue 21	End of "Shopping in Kensington" Batten No. 1 dim to B.O.	(Page 56)

ACT II SCENE 4. Interior. Spring evening, as Act I, Scene 1
To open: Batten No. 1 at ¼

Cue 22	TOM kisses VICTORIA Batten No. 1 fade to B.O.	(Page 56)
Cue 23	When TOM exits, and the armchair is struck Batten No. 2 snaps on FULL	(Page 57)
Cue 24	Author's Flat Gauze flies away Batten No. 1 snaps on FULL	(Page 57)
Cue 25	End of "Taken for a Ride" Battens No. 1 and 2 snap B.O.	(Page 59)

ACT II, SCENE 5. Exterior. Evening
To open: Batten No. 1 (blue and straw circuits only for moonlight effect) at ½

ACT II, SCENE 6. Exterior. Night
To open: Battens No. 1, 2 and 3 (blue and straw circuits only) at ¼
Property fittings ON

Cue 26	DANCERS enter Battens No. 1, 2 and 3 build to ½	(Page 62)

ACT II, SCENE 7. Exterior. Night
To open: Batten No. 1 remains at ½

Cue 27	VICTORIA: ". . . make myself conspicuous." Batten No. 1 dim to B.O.	(Page 64)
Cue 28	VICTORIA and TOM exit Batten No. 1 (blues only) build to ¼	(Page 65)
Cue 29	YOUNG MOTHER smiles at audience Batten No. 1 snap B.O.	(Page 65)

ACT II, SCENE 8. Interior. Night
To open: Battens No. 1, 2 and 3 on FULL

Cue 30	End of "Waiting for our Daughter" Battens No. 1, 2 and 3 slow dim to B.O.	(Page 69)
Cue 31	Following a slight pause after Cue 29 Batten No. 1 (blues only) build to ¼	
Cue 32	VICTORIA: "It's all right. I'm here." Batten No. 2 (blues only) build to ¼	(Page 69)
Cue 33	After VICTORIA "I'll find a light." Battens No. 1, 2 and 3 (all circuits) snap up FULL	(Page 69)
Cue 34	TOM: "Dear stranger." Battens No. 1, 2 and 3, all blue and straw circuits fade OUT (pinks remain FULL)	(Page 73)
Cue 35	Author's Flat Gauze drops in Batten No. 1 returns to FULL	(Page 73)

ACT II, SCENE 9. Exterior. Full lighting
    Battens No. 1, 2 and 3 at FULL
    Property fittings ON
    Star-cloth LIT
    No Cues
    Remain to end of play

PLOT FOR NUMBER 1 FOLLOWING SPOT

ACT I, SCENE 1 (Author's Flat)
To open: ON *Tom* (R) *and follow*

Cue 1	VICTORIA: "And the lighting shows it's day." *Snap* OUT	(Page 3)
Cue 2	End of "Tra, La, La." ON *Tom and follow*	(Page 4)
Cue 3	TOM: ".'. . . expression of Mr Gilchrist's success." *Leave Tom. Pick up Mr Gilchrist on his entrance,* R, *and follow*	(Page 6)
Cue 4	TOM: "The music drifts past him." *Iris or dim* OUT	(Page 6)

ACT I, SCENE 4 (Battersea Park)
To open: ON *Walter* (*up* RC) *and follow*

Cue 5	End of "I'm Away" *Snap* OUT	(Page 18)
Cue 6	TOM: "Several long hours." ON *Victoria on her entrance,* R, *and follow across stage. Immediately*	(Page 20)
Cue 7	VICTORIA exits ON *Tom and follow*	(Page 20)
Cue 8	End of "Follow That Girl" *Snap* OUT	(Page 22)

ACT I, SCENE 6 (Albert Bridge)
To open: OFF

Cue 9	At end of scene (Running Tabs close) ON *Mrs Gilchrist and follow*	(Page 29)
Cue 10	MRS GILCHRIST exits ON *Bystanders*	(Page 29)
Cue 11	End of "Lost, Stolen or Strayed" *Snap* OUT *Fit No. 15 filter* (*peacock blue*)	(Page 29)

ACT I, SCENE 7 (Aquarium)
To open: On *Victoria on her entrance,* R, *and follow*

Cue 12	KEEPER: "Get back in your tank." *Snap* OUT *Remove filter*	(Page 30)
Cue 13	VICTORIA: "I wonder what saved me." ON *Tom on his entrance,* L, *and follow*	(Page 30)

Cue 14	Tom's exit *Leave Tom. Pick up Victoria and follow. Immediately:*	(Page 31)
Cue 15	When Victoria rejoins the Keeper *Leave Victoria. Pick up Keeper and follow*	(Page 31)
Cue 16	Victoria and Keeper exit On *Mermaid Tank*, up c	(Page 31)
Cue 17	Black backing behind gauze flies away *Snap* Out	(Page 31)
Cue 18	Gauze flies away On *Mermaids and follow*	(Page 31)
Cue 19	Mermaids return to tank *Snap* Out	(Page 33)
Cue 20	Keeper: "Much more to it than that." On *Keeper and follow*	(Page 33)
Cue 21	End of "Mermaid Scales" *Snap* Out	(Page 35)

Act I, Scene 8 (City Centre)
To open: On *Tom* (c) *and follow*
   Remain to end of Act

Act II, Scene 1 (Author's Flat)
To open: On *Tom* (r)

Cue 22	When Batten No 1 dims to B.O. *Snap* Out	(Page 41)
Cue 23	Tom returns as policeman On *Tom and follow*	(Page 41)
Cue 24	Tom exits *Snap* Out	(Page 41)
Cue 25	Wilberforce: "What, what, what?" On *Wilberforce and follow*	(Page 42)
Cue 26	Wilberforce exits *Snap* Out	(Page 43)

Act II, Scene 4 (Author's Flat)
To open: On *Victoria* (r) *and follow*

Cue 27	Author's Flat Gauze flies away *Snap* Out	(Page 57)

Act II, Scene 5 (Running Tabs)
To open: On *Tom on his entrance,* l, *and follow*

Cue 28	Tom exits *Snap* Out	(Page 60)

Act II, Scene 6 (City Centre)
To open: Off

Cue 29	As VICTORIA enters (up R) ON *Victoria and follow throughout*	(Page 61)

ACT II, SCENE 7
    Remain with Victoria

Cue 30	VICTORIA exits *Snap* OUT	(Page 65)
Cue 31	YOUNG MOTHER enters R ON *Young Mother and follow*	(Page 65)
Cue 32	YOUNG MOTHER smiles at audience *Snap B.O.*	(Page 65)

ACT II, SCENE 8 (Gilchrist Drawing-room)
To open: ON *Mr Gilchrist* (RC) *and follow*

Cue 33	MR GILCHRIST exits *Snap* OUT	(Page 69)
Cue 34	TOM: "Dear stranger." ON *Tom and follow*	(Page 73)
Cue 35	TOM exits Return C *stage for general lighting during* FINALE *and* CURTAIN CALLS	(Page 74)

PLOT FOR NUMBER 2 FOLLOWING SPOT

ACT I, SCENE 1 (Author's Flat)
To open: OFF

Cue 1	VICTORIA enters L ON *Victoria and follow*	(Page 1)
Cue 2	End of "Tra, La, La" *Iris or dim* OUT	(Page 4)
Cue 3	VICTORIA moves up stage to the piano ON *Victoria and follow*	(Page 5)
Cue 4	TOM: ". . . proud and unsmiling" *Leave Victoria. Pick up Tom and follow*	(Page 6)
Cue 5	TOM: "The music drifts past him." *Iris or dim* OUT	(Page 6)

ACT I, SCENE 4 (Battersea Park)
To open: OFF

Cue 6	CORA enters ON *Cora on her entrance*, R, *and follow*	(Page 15)
Cue 7	End of "I'm Away". *Snap* OUT	(Page 18)

ACT I, SCENE 6 (Albert Bridge)
To open: OFF

Cue 8	At end of scene (Running Tabs close) ON *Cora and follow*	(Page 29)
Cue 9	CORA exits ON *Bystanders*	(Page 29)
Cue 10	End of "Lost, Stolen or Strayed" *Snap* OUT	(Page 29)

ACT I, SCENE 7 (Aquarium)
To open: OFF

Cue 11	KEEPER enters ON *Keeper on his entrance*, R, *and follow*	(Page 30)
Cue 12	KEEPER: "Get back in your tank." *Take in Victoria and follow her*	(Page 30)
Cue 13	VICTORIA and KEEPER exit ON *Mermaid Tank, up* C	(Page 31)
Cue 14	Black backing behind gauze flies away *Snap* OUT	(Page 31)
Cue 15	Gauze flies away ON *Mermaids and follow*	(Page 31)

Cue 16	MERMAIDS return to tank *Snap* OUT	(Page 33)
Cue 17	KEEPER: ". . . much more to it than that." ON *Victoria and follow*	(Page 33)
Cue 18	End of "Mermaid Scales" *Snap* OUT	(Page 35)

ACT I, SCENE 8 (City Centre)
To open: OFF

Cue 19	VICTORIA enters ON *Victoria on her entrance, up* L, *and follow* *Remain to end of Act*	(Page 38)

ACT II, SCENE 1 (Author's Flat)
To open: OFF

Cue 20	MRS GILCHRIST: "Lights, please." ON *Mrs Gilchrist* (LC) *and follow*	(Page 40)
Cue 21	MRS GILCHRIST exits *Snap* OUT *Wait there for—*	(Page 41)
Cue 22	TANCRED and WILBERFORCE enter ON *Tancred and Wilberforce on their entrance,* R, *and follow*	(Page 41)
Cue 23	WILBERFORCE: "What, what, what?" *Now follow Tancred only*	(Page 42)
Cue 24	TANCRED exits *Snap* OUT	(Page 43)

ACT II, SCENE 4 (Author's Flat)
To open: OFF

Cue 25	TOM enters ON *Tom on his entrance,* L, *and follow*	(Page 56)
Cue 26	TOM: "I wish you joy if it . . ." *Snap* OUT	(Page 57)

ACT II, SCENE 6 (City Centre)
To open: OFF

Cue 27	VICTORIA: "How long have you been standing there?" ON *Tom* (C) *and follow throughout*	(Page 61)

ACT II, SCENE 7
Remain with TOM

Cue 28	TOM exits *Snap* OUT	(Page 64)
Cue 29	TOM re-enters ON *Tom and follow*	(Page 64)
Cue 30	TOM exits *Snap* OUT	(Page 65)

ACT II, SCENE 8 (Gilchrist Drawing-room)
To open ON *Mrs Gilchrist* (C) *and follow*
Cue 31 MRS GILCHRIST exits (Page 69)
Snap OUT
Cue 32 TOM: "Dear stranger." (Page 73)
ON *Victoria and follow*
Cue 33 VICTORIA exits (Page 74)
Return C *stage for general lighting during* FINALE *and* CURTAIN CALLS

HANGING PLOT

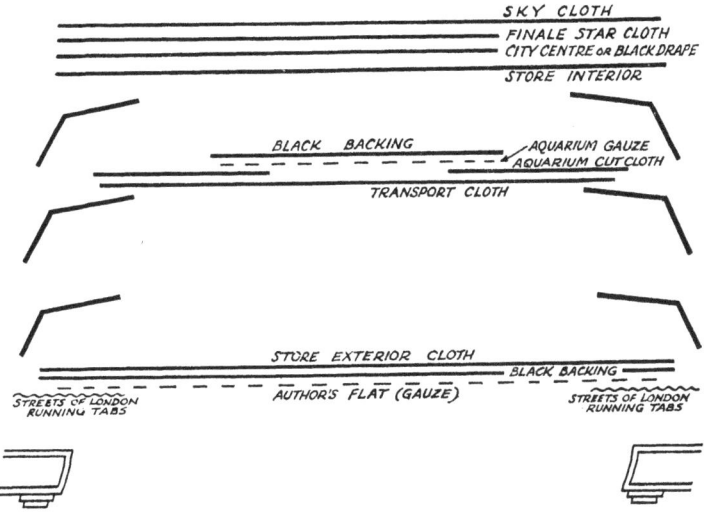

FLIES PLOT

In the following Plot, the Running Tabs are assumed to occupy line 1. Lighting Battens, Borders and Legs, where used, remain unaltered throughout, and the lines employed for these features are not numbered.

ACT I

To open: In Author's Flat Gauze (line 2)
Black Backing for Gauze (line 3)
Skycloth (line 12)
STAND BY HOUSE CURTAIN

ACT I, SCENE 1

Cue 1	VICTORIA: ". . . and then a blank page."	(Page 2)
	TAKE OUT Black Backing (line 3)	
Cue 2	TOM (*singing*) "Their dresses show it's summer."	(Page 3)
	TAKE OUT Author's Flat Gauze (line 2)	

ACT I, SCENE 6
Cue 3   When RUNNING TABS close at end of Albert Bridge
           scene   (Page 29)
              DROP IN   Aquarium Cut Cloth (line 6)
                         Aquarium Gauze (line 7)
                         Black Backing for Gauze (line 8)

ACT I, SCENE 7
Cue 4   VICTORIA and the KEEPER turn away from the
           Mermaid Tank   (Page 31)
              TAKE OUT Black Backing for Gauze (line 8)
Cue 5   MERMAIDS (*singing*) "By breaking the glass and
           screaming."   (Page 32)
              TAKE OUT Aquarium Gauze (line 7)
Cue 6   MERMAIDS return to tank and finish musical number
           "Three Victorian Mermaids"   (Page 33)
              DROP IN   Aquarium Gauze (line 7)
                         Black Backing for Gauze (line 8)
Cue 7   RUNNING TABS close during "Mermaid Scales"   (Page 35)
              TAKE OUT Aquarium Cut Cloth (line 6)
                        Aquarium Gauze (line 7)
                        Black Backing for Gauze (line 8)
                        Skycloth (line 12)
              DROP IN   City Centre Cloth (or Black Drape) (line 10)
           STAND BY HOUSE CURTAIN

ACT II
To open: IN Author's Flat Gauze (line 2)
              Black Backing for Gauze (line 3)
              Store Interior (line 9)
           STAND BY HOUSE CURTAIN

ACT II, SCENE 1
Cue 8   RUNNING TABS close   (Page 41)
              TAKE OUT Author's Flat Gauze (line 2)
                        Black Backing for Gauze (line 3)

ACT II, SCENE 2
Cue 9   In BLACK-OUT at end of scene   (Page 53)
              DROP IN   Store Exterior (line 4)
              TAKE OUT Store Interior (line 9)

ACT II, SCENE 3
Cue 10 In BLACK-OUT at end of scene   (Page 56)
              DROP IN   Author's Flat Gauze (line 2)
                        Black Backing for Gauze (line 3)

ACT II, SCENE 4
Cue 11   At OPENING of scene (Page 56)
          TAKE OUT Store Exterior (line 4)
          DROP IN Transport Cloth (line 5)
                  City Centre Cloth (line 10)
Cue 12   VICTORIA: "It'll get rid of them." (Page 56)
          TAKE OUT Black Backing to Gauze (line 3)
Cue 13   TAXIMAN: "Jump in, Lady." (Page 57)
          TAKE OUT Author's Flat Gauze (line 2)

ACT II, SCENE 5
Cue 14   At OPENING of scene (Page 59)
          TAKE OUT Transport Cloth (line 5)

ACT II, SCENE 7
Cue 15   At OPENING of scene (Page 63)
          TAKE OUT City Centre Cloth (line 10)
          (but if this is Black Drape LEAVE IN)
          DROP IN Skycloth (line 12) if Black Drape not
                  available

ACT II, SCENE 8
Cue 16   End of "Lovely Meeting You at Last" Reprise (Page 73)
          DROP IN Author's Flat Gauze (line 2)
                  Black Backing for Gauze (line 3)
          TAKE OUT Skycloth (line 12), or Black Drape (line 10)
          DROP IN Finale Star Cloth (line 11)
Cue 17   When RUNNING TABS closed (Page 74)
          TAKE OUT Author's Flat Gauze (line 2)
                  Black Backing for Gauze (line 3)
          STAND BY HOUSE CURTAIN

RUNNING TABS PLOT

ACT I
To open: Running Tabs OPEN

ACT I, SCENE 2
Cue 1   STAGE-HAND exits with stool   (Page 14)
         CLOSE *Running Tabs*

ACT I, SCENE 3
Cue 2   MR GILCHRIST exits L   (Page 15)
         OPEN *Running Tabs*

ACT I, SCENE 4
Cue 3   MR GILCHRIST and TOM exit R   (Page 24)
         CLOSE *Running Tabs*

ACT I, SCENE 5
Cue 4   TOM exits down L   (Page 25)
         OPEN *Running Tabs*

ACT I, SCENE 6
Cue 5   COMPANY (*singing*) "And jumped right in."   (Page 29)
         CLOSE *Running Tabs*
Cue 6   BYSTANDERS exit in B.O. at end of "Lost, Stolen, or Strayed"   (Page 29)
         OPEN *Running Tabs*

ACT I, SCENE 7
Cue 7   KEEPER (*singing*) "When you marry I will give you a trousseau."   (Page 35)
         CLOSE *Running Tabs*

ACT I, SCENE 8
Cue 8   When City Centre scene set   (Page 35)
         OPEN *Running Tabs*

ACT II
To open: Running Tabs OPEN

ACT II, SCENE 1
Cue 9   VICTORIA exits   (Page 41)
         CLOSE *Running Tabs*
Cue 10   COCKNEYS (*singing*) "Hand in hand."   (Page 43)
         OPEN *Running Tabs*

ACT II, SCENE 3
Cue 10A   (Optional) During "Shopping in Kensington"   (Page 56)
CLOSE *Running Tabs if required for scene change*

ACT II, SCENE 4
Cue 10B   As scene begins   (Page 56)
OPEN *Running Tabs*
Cue 11   End of "Taken for a Ride"   (Page 59)
CLOSE *Running Tabs*

ACT II, SCENE 5
Cue 12   TOM (*singing*) "Lovely Meeting You at Last" (end of 1st Refrain)   (Page 60)
OPEN *Running Tabs*

ACT II, SCENE 6
Cue 13   End of Chorus Reprise "Lovely Meeting You at Last"   (Page 63)
CLOSE *Running Tabs*

ACT II, SCENE 7
Cue 14   Lights Black-Out   (Page 65)
OPEN *Running Tabs*

ACT II, SCENE 8
Cue 15   Music to "Evening in London" Begins   (Page 74)
CLOSE *Running Tabs*
Cue 16   TOM and VICTORIA exit L   (Page 74)
OPEN *Running Tabs*

EFFECTS PLOT

ACT I
No Cues

ACT II, SCENE 7

Cue 1	YOUNG MOTHER enters wheeling pram *Effect: Baby crying loudly*	(Page 65)
Cue 2	YOUNG MOTHER: "Oh, *shut up!*" *Stop effect instantly*	(Page 65)

Character costumes and wigs used in the performance of plays contained in French's Acting Edition may be obtained from Messrs CHARLES H. FOX LTD, 184 High Holborn, London, W.C.1.

MADE AND PRINTED IN GREAT BRITAIN BY
LATIMER TREND AND CO. LTD, PLYMOUTH
MADE IN ENGLAND

www.ingramcontent.com/pod-product-compliance
Ingram Content Group UK Ltd.
Pitfield, Milton Keynes, MK11 3LW, UK
UKHW021843210426
5322IPUK00022B/444